W9-AYY-007

Father's
Day Creek

Father's Day Creek

*Fly fishing, fatherhood
and the last best place on Earth*

Dan Rodricks

*Foreword by fly fishing legend
Lefty Kreh*

Apprentice
House Press
Loyola University Maryland

Copyright © 2019 by Dan Rodricks

All rights reserved. No part of this book may be reproduced or transmitted in any form or by any means, electronic or mechanical, including photocopy, recording, or any information storage and retrieval system, without prior permission from the publisher (except by reviewers who may quote brief passages).

First Edition

Hardcover ISBN: 978-1-62720-219-0
Paperback ISBN: 978-1-62720-220-6
Ebook ISBN: 978-1-62720-221-3

Printed in the United States of America

Acquisitions Editor: Olivia Airhart
Design by Olivia Airhart
Illustrations by Julia M. Rodricks
Promotion plan by Rachael Miller

Published by Apprentice House Press

Apprentice House Press
Loyola University Maryland
4501 N. Charles Street
Baltimore, MD 21210
410.617.5265 • 410.617.2198 (fax)
www.ApprenticeHouse.com
info@ApprenticeHouse.com

For Lillian, Nick and Julia

Introduction

Where would you want to spend your final hours? How would you want to remember life on Earth? Maybe you'd want to be at home in bed, or perhaps in a beautiful temple or stained-glass cathedral, maybe in a library or museum surrounded by great works, perhaps in a favorite place from childhood. I would want to leave by way of Father's Day Creek. It's a freestone river that runs through a verdant gorge in Pennsylvania, sheltered by hemlocks, and it seems remote and pristine, though it is neither. For me, Father's Day Creek has become what Chief Joseph of the Nez Perce called a "spirit-home" and, because of my faith in its resilient beauty, I consider it The Last Best Place on Earth. I hope this book gets you to think about your own "spirit-home," or Last Best Place, or maybe it will convince you to go out to the woods to claim one before it's too late. I recommend that everyone take emotional possession of a place, away from the rush of modern life, where you can feel at home and at peace – a place that deepens your love of the natural world, makes you happy to be alive and downright militant about saving our messed-up planet.

I found my little bit of paradise through fly fishing, and a lot of this book is about that form of angling, how and why I came to it and passed my passion on to my son. The book meanders like the creek of its title – an alias I gave the place years ago – and along the way I share some experiences and observations about nature, about friends and family, about being a son and becoming a father, all tied in some way to fishing.

In his poem, "The Pasture," Robert Frost invites us to join him as he heads out for farm chores. "I sha'n't be gone long," he says. "You come too." And the hope, same as here, is that you'll find something new and feel refreshed.

I do not pretend to be an expert at fly fishing or parenthood, but if you're thinking about getting into one or the other, or both, you might pick up a few pointers. If you've been there and done that already, then I offer this book as a way of comparing notes on fishing and fatherhood.

The story-within-the-story is about the three hours of Father's Day morning – Sunday, June 18, 2000 – when I fished the creek, by myself, reached a milestone and had an epiphany about fishing and its larger meanings. I give an accounting of that adventure with time-stamped installments that describe my fishing rituals and my relationship with the creek and its surroundings. In the years when I fished Father's Day regularly, and usually alone, I kept a journal, but not an hour-by-hour one. So I've done my best to recreate what I did that memorable morning and what happened on my last cast before breakfast.

Because I am a journalist and consider myself a conservationist, part of the book reports what I've learned about efforts to restore Eastern trout streams to their historic best. Father's Day Creek is one such place, an environmental success story, having recovered as a healthy wild trout habitat after years of indiscriminate overfishing by anglers who waded into it looking for supper.

Some parts of the essays in this book, including one on the late Mike Flanagan of the Baltimore Orioles, first appeared in *The Baltimore Sun*, where I've been a news columnist since 1979. The shared 5th-floor newsroom of *The Sun* and *Evening Sun,* then on Calvert Street in downtown Baltimore, is where I first met Bernard "Lefty" Kreh. He was the morning Sun's outdoors editor and already a globe-trotting fly fishing legend – a casting instructor to presidents and movie stars – though I had no awareness of that until, more than a decade later, I opened up a spring catalogue to find a photo of Lefty endorsing a fly rod. I kept in touch with Lefty over the years, after he left *The Sun*, and at one point he gave me and my son, Nick, a casting lesson that was as hilarious and as bewildering as it was instructive and helpful.

In the summer of 2017, when Lefty was 92, I asked him to consider writing the foreword for this book. He agreed. But within a few months, he had become ill and weak and, in both an email and phone call, Lefty apologized for not being able to complete the foreword. Fortunately, by the following January, he was on the phone again, and feeling better. He invited me to his house and offered to dictate his contribution. I sat in his living room with my laptop computer and typed along as Lefty, breathing with the help of an oxygen tank, told stories of fishing, fatherhood and his "spirit-home" on the Potomac River. He approved the final draft of the foreword just a few weeks before he died after a long and beautiful life.

– December 2018

Foreword

The idea of Dan Rodricks' book really hit home for me. I have fished on the fly in 22 countries, and I have fished with some famous people – Ted Williams, Tom Brokaw, Fidel Castro, Ernest Hemingway – and I enjoyed sharing my casting knowledge with many of them. But my favorite memories from fishing days come from a place close to where I grew up in Maryland. They involve my son, Larry. But they do not involve a fly rod.

Back in the 1950s, when I owned a Model A Ford and Larry was just five years old, we would drive to a place on the Potomac River known as Twin Rocks to fish with spinning rods. The spot was between Lander and Point of Rocks, on the Maryland side. My family used to have a cabin near there, and we spent a good part of each summer on the river.

A fellow named Buggs Cross, who lived there with his wife, rented boats. Few people had outboard motors in those days, so I poled one of Buggs' boats. Larry and I found the deepest hole well upstream from where most people were willing to pole. It was called Twin Rocks because there were two boulders, identical in size, that tilted out of the water.

The pool was just above the Twins. It was about 75 yards across and 100 yards long. It could be 12 feet deep at times, and it was loaded with all kinds of fish. We anchored the boat on the pool, and Larry and I fished for catfish, using shrimp for bait, which was only 20 cents a pound back then. It was not unusual to catch 25 to 30 catfish under 15 inches.

It was a wonderful experience, and we felt like we had the place to ourselves.

Larry and I started fishing with minnows, and we would catch smallmouth bass, some as large as three to four pounds. Then we discovered carp fishing. Buggs showed me how to make carp dough with a pint of water, a tablespoon of sugar and some vanilla extract, a bag of dry flour and corn bread mix, and one packet of strawberry Jell-o. Buggs would cook that up and stir in the ingredients in a certain way so that, when it cooled and he rolled the dough balls, they would bounce. Most importantly, they would not come off the hook when we cast our lines. We caught a lot of carp that way, many between 10 and 15 pounds, but some up to 30 pounds.

I truly enjoyed fishing with Larry, but there are days when God does not like your son.

I was working for Fenwick Rod Co. at the time and had a Fenwick fly rod for bass fishing. I also had a new stainless steel thermos that I really loved. A friend of mine worked in a factory where they would dip products in thick rubber coating, and I asked him to do that to the thermos. That way, I could carry it in my aluminum canoe and it would not make noise. Plus, the stainless steel cup would not burn my lips when I went to sip my coffee. I loved that thermos. I had saved up for it.

But, as I said, there are days when God does not like your son.

We were fishing at Twin Rocks again, this time in my aluminum jon boat. Larry decided he was going to drink some coffee. When he went to open my precious thermos, it slipped out of his hands and went to the bottom of the pool. The same day, he stepped on my Fenwick rod and snapped it. And then he fell in the river, and I had to take him over to the bank and build a fire to dry off his clothes.

Well, I got through all that without killing him. We got back to the ramp and put the jon boat on the roof of my Ford. As we were driving home, Larry leaned against my shoulder. He was feeling bad so I started a little conversation with him. "Well, son," I said, "you know, in a couple more years, you're gonna drive this car, just like me, and you're gonna pole the boat, just like me, and your dad is gonna sit up there and fish just like you do now."

And he looked up at me, with those innocent eyes, and said, "Dad, does that mean I can cuss you, too?"

The years went by, and we'd go up to Twin Rocks and fish in Indian summer, those calm days in October when the trees along the Potomac were all lit up. It was a ritual for us to fish up there two or three times a year.

But then, life happens. Larry went into the Army, and he got married.

And, unfortunately, over the years, the Potomac has suffered from farming and development upstream, a lot insecticides and herbicides. Years ago, on a summer evening, millions of hatching White Miller mayflies fell to the surface where the fish gorged on them. Not anymore. We used to hear thousands of big brown toads at sunset going *grah grah grah*. But I haven't heard that sound in 30 or 35 years.

Still, I continued going to Twin Rocks until I hit my 90s.

I have fished from the Amazon to Iceland, from salt flats to salmon rivers. But my favorite trip takes me to my place at Twin Rocks on an Indian summer day. I make my carp dough, my lunch and coffee – and pack some Fig Newtons for dessert – and get on the road. I get up to the pool and just sit there in the boat, and it brings back all those memories of good times with Larry.

My wife, Ev, once said to me, as I was packing my lunch: "You always go there by yourself. Why? Why not take someone with you?"

And I said, "When I'm up there by myself, I think about this place that was a secret for our son and me for so many years." I like to go there and, even if I don't catch fish – something that was impossible to imagine years ago – I enjoy all the memories that special place created.

It's important that we find these special places and claim them as our own – if not in title, at least in our hearts – and that we do what we can to take care of them for the next generation.

Lefty Kreh
Cockeysville, Maryland,
February 2018

Father's Day Creek

I can hear him now: "All that for that?" I can pretty much see him, too, in his khaki trousers and white T-shirt. He's standing in the small clearing by the honeysuckle thicket on the banks of the creek I love. My father is watching me fish in the way I have chosen to fish in the years since his death, a way that must seem odd and foolish to him: With a fly rod and tiny lures fashioned from feathers and animal hair to look like the bugs that finicky trout eat. I have been standing knee-deep in the river and casting flies for the better part of an hour. I have hooked only this one fish, and it's small. As I play it out of the fast current in the middle of the creek, I can hear Iron Joe laugh: "Oh, boy, Danny!" I extend my wood-handle net for a trout that's all green, yellow and white with brown spots, about 10 inches of God's glory. I hold the trout in my hand for a moment so that Iron Joe might appreciate it on this Father's Day, the 14th since his death in 1986. But he only laughs: "All that for that?" And when I ease the little fish back into the river, my father laughs harder, turns away, shakes his head and disappears into the woods.

I am the only man in the whole wide world who calls it Father's Day Creek. You won't find that name in any guidebook or atlas. Don't bother Googling it. Father's Day Creek is the alias I gave it, my way of disguising the stream to save it from an onslaught of humans with fishing rods and kayaks. I want no part of promoting the place. I just want to tell you about it because you should know that such a place exists. You will probably want to go there, especially if you enjoy fishing for trout as much as I do. But I am sworn to secrecy. I can describe the place and tell you why I like it so much. I just can't give you the map coordinates.

I call Father's Day Creek the Last Best Place on Earth, and if that sounds grandiose, I offer no apology, only explanation.

For the sake of sanity and soul, everyone should have a place away from The Everything Else of modern life, a spot in the outdoors that can serve as a personal sanctuary and, with a squint of your eye, provide a glimpse of the long-ago. The Last Best Place is where you would want to be if you knew the world would end tomorrow. It's how you would want to remember life on Earth.

Don't worry if you have not designated your Last Best Place; there's no requirement that you do so. And unless the subject came up after a few drinks around a campfire – "So where would you like to be when the world comes to and end?" – you've probably never even been asked about this before.

But now that I've presented the idea, with the intention of telling you about Father's Day Creek, I bet you can identify and describe your Last Best Place. I bet you know exactly what I mean – that place you visit once a year, if not physically, at least in memory, a small piece of the planet you consider your own. I'm not talking necessarily about a tourist hot spot, a spectacular canyon or mountain range in a national park. I'm talking about a more intimate place that has personal meaning – a spot beneath a tree you've long admired, a simple boulder along a trail with a mesmirizing view, or a quiet clearing in woods, maybe a familiar slice of lakefront, or an acre of beach you knew as a child. You don't have to own the place – in fact, you probably don't – but you've always felt a strong, oddly familiar connection to it. I've come to suspect that, at certain moments in life, something in the primal brain takes over and triggers a deep-rooted sensation, as if the ancestors inside us have been stirred awake by something that looks, sounds or smells familiar to them. It could be the aroma of venison cooking on an open fire. It could be the sound of wind in a treeline. It could be the sight of a rocky shore. There's been some speculation, and even some research, about DNA holding the memories of ancestors, the idea being that we've inherited the effects of long-ago experiences from all those people we never knew, the ancients who rest at the roots of our family trees. Maybe something like that is at work when we visit and revisit these special places.

When I go to Father's Day Creek, and when I'm standing in it with my fly rod, I consider it to be absolutely perfect, untouched, frozen in time – perhaps as it was in the age of the Delaware Tribe – with all the horrors of the human epoch yet to take place. No countries, no conquest, no wars, no calamity, everything as it was after the big ice receded and the trees started to grow among the boulders that the glaciers left behind.

I step through the high weeds and push through the brush along the banks of Father's Day Creek and, if there is nothing to disturb my ear, such as the motor of a homeowner's electric leaf blower or the snorts of distant tractor-trailers, if all I hear are the squawks of blue jays and crows and, below me, the constant rush of the stream, then I am in paradise, and I have paradise to myself.

The place looks so pristine and inviting, so constant and enduring, I sometimes feel unworthy of it, as if an intruder, a riparian peeping Tom who should just catch a quick glimpse and leave. There is nothing here but the real world of trees, clear water, rocks as old as time, flickering birds, dancing insects and rising trout. There is hardly ever any evidence of the world beyond the road where I park my car – the congested and trashy, confusing and crazy, coughing and fuming, fossil-burning, nattering, head-banging world of 24-7 news and non-stop noise. Not in Father's Day Creek. There's nothing like that here, only profound tranquility. To pull out a cell phone to take a call or to read a tweet from the human world would be sacrilege.

Bill Burton, one of my late fishing companions, gave me a little book of Native American wisdom, something he used to retrieve from his vest and read when the fishing was slow. There was a quote from Chief Joseph of the Nez Perce: "We were taught to believe that the Great Spirit sees and hears everything, and that he never forgets, and that hereafter he will give every man a spirit-home according to his deserts." I have decreed Father's Day Creek my spirit-home, in the hope that the Great Spirit will grant me a campsite along its banks in the hereafter. I am not kidding. I actually have these thoughts when I'm standing in the stream waving my fly rod. Another native expression, this one supposedly from Crazy Horse of the Lakota, goes: "Today is a good day to die." While you could take that to be a warrior's credo – the desire to die an honorable death for a worthy cause – I take it to mean satisfaction with having lived life well and a way of giving thanks for accumulating minimal regrets. I say it to myself when I arrive in Father's Day Creek, before I start fishing: "Today is a good day to die." I know it seems strange, but that's my ritual. Holy places demand ritual.

Father's Day Creek is a valley stream in Pennsylvania that I have visited two or three times a year for the last 25 years, but it lives in my imagination, too. It is always with me. I carry it in my mind the way a parent carries a picture of a child in a wallet.

I take it with me everywhere I go, even to other trout streams. I can visit the creek anytime I like. I can relive the jaw-dropping moment, on that same Father's Day in 2000 when I imagined my father watching me, when something happened that made my journey as a fly fisher complete.

You will find that story downstream of where we are right now, along with my accounts of other great times on the creek – for instance, the May afternoon when my son, who had just graduated from college, was with me for an amazing hatch of large mayflies that brought numerous trout to the surface for lunch, a primal, splashy feeding frenzy that went on for more than an hour. I also recall easily my encounter with a brawny buck crossing the stream, and a mute swan rising from it.

I can walk and wade along 2,000 yards of creek and not see anything that makes me angry or depressed – not a scrap of evidence of the human world: No beer cans or bottles or plastic shopping bags, no tires, cigarette butts or nests of discarded fishing line. The creek flows big and strong in the spring and carries with it loads of debris from upstream, but it is mostly natural detritus from fallen trees and uprooted bushes. Sometimes I spot evidence of human life – a piece of old barn siding, porcelain insulators from a farmer's electric fence – but that's rare. One time I discovered a busted laptop computer in the bottom of the stream, just below the one-lane bridge near where I park my car. I figured some CIA agent, having downloaded the contents of the hard drive, tossed it from his black SUV as he passed through.

Absurd as it might sound to title attorneys, I soon came to believe that Father's Day Creek belonged to me. I was convinced that the happy circumstances of life had delivered me to this hallowed place: Marrying a woman whose parents owned a weekend-and-retirement home near the stream, having their neighbor invite me to fish there all I liked, and having other anglers give up on the place and leave it to me after the commonwealth stopped stocking the creek with hatchery-raised trout. The creek and I were meant for each other, and we hit it off almost from the beginning.

Fly fishing and Father's Day Creek came into my life at almost the same time. They both revived my interest in fishing. I had taken a long hiatus from angling for a bunch of reasons: Once I moved from New England to Maryland, the Chesapeake Bay seemed like the obvious place to fish, but I did not own a boat, and you need to be on a boat to fish the bay. I also lost interest in killing fish – my father's kind of fishing, fishing for food – so I took a pass on fishing the freestone rivers and creeks stocked with trout in the spring. Put-and-take fishing – the state puts the trout in rivers and, two weeks later, you can catch and take up to five of them a day – did not strike me as particularly sporting. I spent one Opening Day of the Maryland trout season standing practically shoulder-to-shoulder in a stocked stream with men and boys who used rubbery, chartreuse-colored fish pellets and Velveeta balls for bait, and I found the whole experience depressing. The other anglers were humorless, even a little surly, because they hated being crowded on the stream. I swore I would never fish that way again, and haven't.

So I took a long break from fishing, accepting the occasional invitation to a charter boat that trolled for hours in the Chesapeake. I pretty much came to dislike that kind of fishing, too. The engines ran all day, a non-stop, headache-inducing chugga-da chugga-da chugga-da. The captain and mate would drop eight to 10 lines with all kinds of heavy-metal contraptions that bounced along the bottom of the bay as the boat moved. When a rockfish, or striped bass, got hooked on one of these rigs, we'd take turns reeling it in. It was all very mechanical, requiring nothing of the angler except the ability to crank the reel until the fish was in the skipper's net, then stand back and open another beer. I no longer fish from trolling charter boats.

As glad as I was to discover fly fishing, I have no specific memory of how or why I got into it. I know it was 1990, the year my son was born, and four years after my father had died and my last severe experience with depression. But I cannot remember who introduced me to it, or where the idea came from. I signed up to take a few casting lessons and started buying gear from a local shop, and within a few months I had a vest, waders, boots, a Scott fly rod and Pflueger Medalist reel – nothing too expensive – and within a few weeks I had a set of new fishing companions, and I was catching brown trout on dry flies in the Big Gunpowder Falls, north of my home in Baltimore. I loved it. I went a little crazy, too. I fished about every three days for two hours at a time, until winter came, and then I fished occasionally in the snow. This kind of fishing – matching artificial flies with the real aquatic insects that trout eat, casting those flies without making a big, fish-spooking splash, and tricking trout into taking them – all of that got into my head and under my skin, and it's the only kind of fishing I've wanted to do since.

I had learned a new skill, caught plenty of trout, and made new friends who also fished on the fly. When I started catching brown trout in Father's Day Creek, near the weekend home of my in-laws, I allowed myself the selfish thought that life probably would not get better. I had become a father. I had become a fly fisher. I had discovered paradise.

So maybe you can understand why I think I found the Last Best Place on Earth, why I consider it my spirit-home, a good place to be on a good day to die.

I rose from bed, made some coffee, and drove from my in-laws' house to the small parking area by the bridge over the creek. The drive to Father's Day Creek takes you through farmland and forest, and then, for the last mile, down a narrow country road into an area that became a new, but not better, place during my years of fishing there. Old houses and barns on farmland that had appeared to be in full retirement gave way to sprawling ranchers with sprawling lawns, cul de sacs, and two to four cars and trucks per household. The farmers were mostly gone. By Father's Day 2000, the biggest crop in the area seemed to be chemically-treated grass. The road had been graded – all the stomach-tickling dips removed – and paved to impervious perfection and to a smooth glide to accommodate commuters who speed out every weekday morning. Some drive an insane two hours to their jobs. The new development – all those wells and septic systems – and the new road made me worry about their combined effect on my favorite creek. Would the wells diminish the flow of spring water into it? Would the septic systems leak and the bacteria seep into it? Summer rainfall on the new road would certainly send filthy, steamy drainage into the creek's naturally cool waters. I harbored these fears – and they are legitimate fears – each time I visited Father's Day Creek. But on the morning of June 18, 2000, I blocked out my concerns about human behavior and focused on finding trout. I had the place to myself.

In case you are wondering about my credentials when it comes to fishing: I have done a lot of it. But I am not the late, great Lefty Kreh, the world-reknown Yoda of fly casting whose years as outdoors editor of *The Baltimore Sun* overlapped several of mine as a reporter and columnist there. I am not a professional angler or guide, and, while I have worked for newspapers for more than 40 years, I was never an outdoors writer. I am just a guy who has done a lot of weekday and weekend fishing, more than he realized until he did an accounting of it, though, it turns out, not as much as he would have liked.

Starting at age six, I fished for sunfish in a little brook in Massachusetts; hornpout, sunfish and bass in a mill pond; migrating herring in a herring run; cod and haddock, conger eel and mackerel in the deep sea off the New England coast; flounder in the bays near Boston, flounder in the Cape Cod Canal and flounder off a wooden bridge in Duxbury, Massachusetts, flounder off the Virginia coast; striped bass (also known as rockfish) near the Chesapeake Bay Bridge, in the Little Choptank River and Tangier Sound; stripers in a tidal creek on Cape Cod; smallmouth bass in the Susquehanna River (Pennsylvania side), shad in the Susquehanna River (Maryland side), shad in a tributary of the Susquehanna; smallmouth bass and rock bass in the Potomac River and the Delaware River; crappie and carp in three reservoirs; brown trout and rainbow trout in a dozen rivers in Pennsylvania, cutthroat trout in the Lamar Valley of Wyoming, rainbow trout in the Madison River of Montana and the Henry's Fork of Idaho, brook trout in three ponds in New Hampshire; landlocked salmon and brown trout in the Androscoggin River (New Hampshire side), smallmouth bass in the Androscoggin River (Maine side); bluefish and speckled trout in the Chesapeake; hybrid rockfish in a Maryland farm pond; three kinds of trout in the rivers of western Maryland – the Casselman, the Savage, the Youghiogheny, the North Branch of the Potomac, Bear Creek, Muddy Creek, Lostland Run and Sideling Creek – and I've fished for bass in the farm ponds of southern Maryland; jack crevalle and snook in the tidal creeks of Florida's Gulf Coast; false albacore off Montauk; bluefish in the surf of the North Carolina coast; and steelhead in the Salmon River in New York. I've caught brown trout in the Battenkill in Vermont.

I once awoke to the squawking of gulls, hundreds of them, on Cape Hatteras, and ran down to the beach to investigate the cause of the racket. It was minutes after sunrise, and a horde of bluefish had invaded the surf, attacking a school of Atlantic herring, chasing them into the shore. The tide had started to recede, stranding dozens of the herring in large, shallow puddles on the beach. My dog, a black collie-retriever mix named Rosie, hovered over one of the puddles, suddenly snapped up one of the silvery herring and ran off with it in her mouth. In the surf, the slaughter continued for another hour: Hundreds, perhaps thousands of bluefish feeding frantically on frantic herring, and the surf smelled of shredded fish. Another man might have instantly run to fetch his surf rod — you can catch a bluefish in its feeding madness with a bare hook, after all — but I stayed and watched a while. It was the blitz of bluefish the local anglers had told us about. I had never seen one. I tried to imagine the first Hatteras native to come upon this sight, way back when, at the dawn of everything. I imagined him running off to alert his tribe, then giving thanks for the feast that had come crashing ashore.

I did not catch fish in all of the places I just listed, but, as my friend Tom "Bush Hog" James used to say: "Fishin' ain't catchin'."

That might sound like a copout — the motto of someone more interested in drinking beer than hooking bass — but Bush Hog was right about fishing. It's about relationships and conversation, about comparing notes on life with others, about relaxing and getting your mind off the raucous world, the one that screams and roars beyond the ridge line above Father's Day Creek.

Now, it's easy to apply Bush Hog's philosophy if you're just sitting in a lawn chair by a pond or an ocean, or straddling a bench in a boat, waiting for a fish to strike your baited hook. It's easier if your style of fishing is sedentary.

Fly fishing, on the other hand, requires lots of informed decision-making, physical dexterity for the cast, concentration and patience. There's no sitting down, either. You have to hike to the good spots, wade into the water when you get there, stand and deliver your fly to a trout that is sipping bugs in the current and, therefore, vulnerable to deceit. I'd be lying if I said fly fishing wasn't about catching. It is. But most of us do not kill the trout we fool into taking our flies. We catch them, look them over, maybe take a picture, and release them. I cast to trout in Father's Day Creek to see if I can trick them into taking my fly, but also to make sure they're still there, that they've not been decimated by poacher or plague. When they don't bite, I get a little worried. I worry that the trout have scattered because the water temperature has been rising with climate change, or that some fellow from the horrid housing development nearby caught (and killed) a bunch of my fish with hooks baited with Velveeta balls, or that something fouled the stream when I wasn't there to protect it. It could also be that I've been fly fishing long enough to have started losing my touch, but I doubt it.

Father's Day Creek is a three-hour drive from Baltimore. I have neither right nor title to a single acre of the woods around it. And yet I consider the little river my own. I have felt protective of it, as if I were the hired riverkeeper, since the first time I set eyes on it.

The course of the river is varied in the most wonderful ways. Water ripples over a river bottom of brown gravel and decomposed leaf and wood, giving it the shade of dark tea. In some places, the water plunges into deep, spooky holes. It cuts sharply through a rock gorge crowned in hemlock. It rolls softly along a steep slope covered with wild rhododendron. There are places where it is no more than 20 feet wide, others where it opens to more than twice that width. In early spring, the current can knock you off your feet as you try to wade. In summer, the flow is greatly reduced but constant, and the water never seems to get warm enough to harm the wild trout that call it home. Light swarms of yellow insects emerge as evening falls in June, and trout rise to eat them. It is a beautiful, life-sustaining river that never seems to show the downstream effects of the usual upstream menaces – erosion from farming, trash from storm drains, an odor from a leaking sewer or waste-water treatment plant. That's why I consider it the Last Best Place.

It sounds like a perfect place, and it almost is. But it almost wasn't. And if there's a lesson in this story, it's at this moment in my telling – where trout meets man, and where man almost won.

Father's Day Creek had a lot going for it, particularly compared to other rivers in the eastern United States. Since colonial times, the forests that served as their shade-providing canopies had been removed, and settlers turned the land into pastures for livestock and fields for crops. The loss of tree canopy exposed more of the river courses to the sun and raised the water temperatures. Erosion from farming, along with the comings and goings of wandering dairy cows, degraded the streams. That is primarily why so many rivers in the East are stocked with trout in the late winter and spring – the waterways become too warm and muddy to sustain the fragile fish for more than a few months each year.

Father's Day Creek was different. It was in good shape; you might even say ideal. Because it was on private land, still protected by a rich forest, and because its source was still clear and cold, long stretches of Father's Day Creek provided a perfect habitat for brook, brown and rainbow trout.

In May of 1993, during a Saturday night supper at my in-laws' weekend home in the mountains, a fellow named Pierre told me about the stream. Pierre was a longtime friend of my wife's family. My father-in-law and Pierre were both natives of France and both chefs in New York City who spent weekends at second homes in the Pennsylvania countryside. When he heard of my interest in fishing, Pierre bragged of his ability to take numerous trout from the nearby stream, and he invited me to join him and his friend, Roger, there the next morning.

I was eager to see the place. I arrived at 8 o'clock on an overcast Sunday morning. Daylight was just starting to seep through the hemlocks, but Roger and Pierre had been fishing for almost two hours. Roger used a white telescopic fishing pole, the kind that river anglers deploy in France. There's no casting involved. You just extend the rod as far as you need to in order to drop your line and baited hook into a spot where the fish are likely to be. Roger wore boots but he had little interest in wading into the creek. He stood on a boulder beneath a large tree, extended his right arm and, still as a statue, held his rod in place until he felt a tug on the line. He slipped the trout he caught into a wicker creel on a shoulder sling.

Pierre wore a flannel shirt and rubber hip boots, and he fished with a spinning rod and a small brass lure shaped like a willow leaf. When he saw me, he grinned broadly and opened his creel – 13 killed, few more than 6 or 7 inches long, several of them wild brown trout.

"You're lucky you don't get arrested," I half-joked.

Most of Pierre's trout were probably under the minimum size required for harvest by the Commonwealth of Pennsylvania. He did not care about this.

"The smaller the sweeter," said the chef in his French accent. "Oh, yeah, the little ones taste the best."

"Yeah, and you have to kill twice as many to make a meal."

He grumbled at my streamside moralizing and walked away, and, tell you the truth, I don't blame him. The last thing he wanted on a carefree morning of fishing was a lecture on fishing ethics. There were several men along the river that day, and just about all were taking full creels of trout, both wild and stocked. The whole scene seemed greedy and depressingly short-sighted to me, and it threw me completely out of the mood for fishing. As a lover of rivers, I had learned enough about trout habitat to recognize what was happening that day: It was the purging of Father's Day Creek.

From what I could tell, judging from Pierre's and Roger's creels and what I saw of other catches, about a third of the fish taken were the small brown trout born in the stream. The other two-thirds were larger, colorless, hatchery-raised rainbow trout. There's a huge difference. The wild browns were natives, and vital to the stream's sustainability; such fish should almost never be harvested from streams in the heavily populated Eastern states. The stocked rainbows, on the other hand, were just temporary visitors, placed in the stream for two reasons – to provide sport for anglers, and supper for their families.

The Commonwealth of Pennsylvania stocks more than three million adult trout annually in more than 700 rivers, mostly the old waterways considered unfit for a year-round wild trout population. But the stocking crews sometimes put hatchery trout in waters, like Father's Day Creek, that are good enough for wild trout to inhabit all year. This is a huge mistake. It's like putting paroled inmates in a nursery school. The rainbows compete for habitat and for food; they bring chaos to a delicately balanced ecosystem and stress the wild brown trout. It's bad fisheries science, a concession to the fish-killers who use baited hooks and who want to catch stocked trout as conveniently and as quickly as possible – preferably in the same place their fathers took them when they were kids. They care more about maintaning their annual rituals and going home with full creels than about preserving a wild trout habitat, and the fisheries managers are pressured to accommodate that demand.

Stocking is an old tradition in the Eastern states. It is a widely accepted practice, and fisheries managers are caught between two forces – people, like me, who think wild trout streams ought to be left alone and the people who could care less about scientific arguments and look forward to fishing for trout in the usual spots every spring. I have always found it remarkable, and regrettable, that the men and boys who came out to fish during what they considered "trout season" did not care to enjoy the experience but for one day or one week all year long, nor did they care to know more about the rivers they fished. They had come to expect things to always be a certain way, even in nature, no matter how contrived the experience. Father's Day Creek was, to the local guys, just an easy-to-access local river loaded with trout from the hatchery trucks. They expected the state to provide them with fish to catch, over a couple of weeks in April, and maybe May, and then they moved on to other activities. They could not imagine another reason to visit the river, or to even give it much thought; to them, the creek was simply a seasonal conveyer of easily harvested protein.

I've reached a point where I think the stocking should just stop in any stream that can hold wild trout. But, of course, such a decision would likely cause a revolt among the nation's two-week trout anglers. I recognize that some streams are just too degraded, or get too warm in summer, to sustain wild trout. The state stocks those waters with trout so that adults and children can have a pleasant experience. Beyond providing that temporary recreation, however, I don't see what good it does. I would rather see states curtail their stocking and put time and money into stream restoration efforts, to improve water quality and create more habitat for trout and other wildlife.

I make no apology for sounding like an elitist in this regard. Fishing is not only about catching. It's about caring for the natural world around you, and having healthy waters for future generations.

Now and then, whenever I encountered a bait angler who seemed open to the conversation, I would explain some of my reasoning and talk about the challenges of catching wild trout all year in good waters, and how that ideal required the angler to stop fishing with bait and to release what's caught. Instead of expecting the state to keep stocking degraded rivers with trout from a hatchery – a costly process that does nothing for the environment – we should work toward getting streams back to their historic best. Do that, and we could fish for trout every month of the year, and have cleaner waters flowing toward our reservoirs, lakes and bays. We might even reach a place where, with enough restored rivers, anglers who wanted to catch for their supper might be able to keep a couple of stream-bred trout. But until we do more to bring back more miles of healthy waters, we're just financing and managing a cooked-up, half-baked system – stocking fish in rivers in spring to satisfy some seasonal craving for recreational fishing. It no longer makes sense.

That was my streamside rap, delivered with friendly discretion whenever it seemed appropriate. I tried to avoid making it sound like a lecture. I don't know if I ever convinced a single angler to change his ways – to give up bait for artificial lures or flies, to leave his creel at home as a decorative vessel for dried flowers, and to practice catch-and-release fishing – but I tried a few times. I tried it with Pierre on Father's Day Creek, but he was closer to my father and father-in-law in age and generational experience. He was a successful gardener who enjoyed harvesting the fruits of his labors, a chef who, like my father-in-law, took pride in preparing and serving good meals. The trout that he caught in Father's Day Creek, whether wild or stocked, were part of his hunter-gatherer mindset, and as long as the state put trout in the river for the taking, Pierre would take them. And he would serve them, if you please, panned-fried in butter, with red potatoes and asparagus, and a glass of chablis.

The invasion of the hatchery-born rainbows was harmful to Father's Day Creek. Dozens of fishermen, armed with lures and worms and little balls of Velveeta, came to its banks and caught them all in a matter of weeks. But here's the thing: Like Pierre and Roger, these anglers made no distinction between the hatchery rainbows and the wild brown trout. They caught everything and took it all, stripping away the population of wild trout whose presence made the river so special. In 1993, I concluded sadly that, without protection by the Commonwealth, the creek would never be restored to its historic best. It would always be a marginal trout stream. It wasn't sewage or erosion that harmed the river. It was short-sighted fisheries management and an indiscriminate harvest.

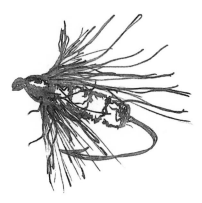

I usually fished the creek on weekends, and always made a point of being there on Father's Day. I prepared by following the same fastidious ritual each time. I parked my car on a grassy spot near the old, one-lane bridge, pleased that no one else had the same idea. I stood outside the car and assembled my two-piece, 4-weight Scott rod and attached the Pfleuger reel. I ran the fly line through the eyes of the rod and checked the last section of the leader, the tippet, to see if it needed to be replaced or lengthened, or at least straighted. If the latter, I squeezed the line through a flat, bell-shaped leather line-straightener attached to my fishing vest. I placed the rod on the roof of my car while I finished setting it up. I attached to the leader about 18 inches of 5X tippet and, to that, an all-purpose fly, a size 16 Adams parachute, and secured it on the hook tender of the rod. Then I dressed for the occasion – chest waders and wading boots, the tan fishing vest that over the years had become way too heavy from acessoriz-ing, with a net attached to a D ring below the soft collar. Then I checked to make sure my car key was in a zippered pocket, and I did this four times. It's a strange habit but a good one; it guarantees I will not lock the key inside my car and spoil a day of fishing waiting for road service. Key secured, I headed for the trail down to the river. I'm a happy man when the trail appears overgrown with bushes and weeds. That means no one else has fished the creek for a good while. It was just that way on Father's Day 2000.

I hope you can understand this feeling of being possessive of a place, of developing a sense of responsibility for it. Ownership is all in my head and my heart. I feel protective of the place, though I live 152 miles away from it and no longer visit as often as I once did. Father's Day Creek is not simply a favorite fishing hole. It is a place I retreat to, in a pilgrimage of the mind, when there's too much sad and bad news in the world, and especially in Baltimore, my adopted hometown. So one of my most valuable possessions is something I do not own. With the East Coast feeling more and more overcrowded and with rural vistas disappearing, I covet a spot that seems isolated and undisturbed, and I hope you know of such a place, or will seek one soon.

Of course, if I gave you the exact location of Father's Day Creek, you could find it on a Google Map and see plenty of houses nearby – including Pierre's and my in-laws' – and a gas station and town center within a couple of miles. In fact, the area has become overdeveloped, with scattered housing and a strip of commercial clutter and grotesque suburbia in the midst of what was all farm country three decades ago.

The land around the creek has not been wilderness for going on 400 years. The trees are descendants of ancestors that fell to the logger's ax long ago. The stream-bred brown trout – what I refer to as "wild trout" – are not a native species. They were introduced after the original inhabitants had been wiped out. The same is true of the small rainbows I sometimes catch; they were introduced to the stream, adapted to it and managed to reproduce. In fact, the only trout that could be considered native are the little brookies; those that swim in Father's Day Creek today are likely the cold-blooded descendants of the brook trout that have survived the intrusions of settlers, loggers, farmers and hunter-gatherers.

I believe this because it fits with a wishful but informed perception of the creek – a stretch of private waters that seemed capable of a robust rebirth if the Commonwealth of Pennsylvania would only stop stocking it with trout, thereby discouraging human visitors. The potential reward seemed great for minimal effort, or no effort at all: If humans would stay away, the stream could be restored and the wild trout could grow in numbers and size. It's what I believed. So I did my part. I stopped fishing in Father's Day Creek. I left it alone. I wanted no part of the pillaging that took place each spring. I fished in other streams designated for catch-and-release fishing, and only with artificial lures and flies. This is one of the things you learn when you take up fly fishing. I do not know a single angler who fishes with a fly rod and kills trout. I am sure there are some out there, but I've yet to meet one. The reason is simple: If everyone who caught trout killed trout there would be no trout left, and every river would have to be stocked with fish from the hatcheries.

My father, of course, would never have understood this. He had been brought up too poor to understand it, and he had lived through a time when fish of all kinds appeared in endless abundance. In 1971, he caught a 36-pound cod off the coast of Massachusetts. That was not a grand-looking fish that deserved to be photographed, then quickly returned to the over-harvested Georges Bank to procreate. To my father, that cod represented a week's worth of baked fish, Portuguese chowder and a pile of fish cakes. My father would not have bothered to fish Father's Day Creek – small water and "dinky fish" – and he would have wondered why I spent so much time there, with so little to show for it.

This idea of claiming a piece of river that does not belong to you comes from boyhood fantasies. I had places I considered my own when I was growing up in a small Massachusetts town south of Boston. One was a fishing hole about 20-feet wide on the downstream side of a small bridge no more than 300 yards from my home. It was on a foul little brook that flowed from Forge Pond, north of the center of town, through woods and past an aluminum foundry owned by a neighborhood family, the Santillis. Years later, I discovered the stream on a map, and with a deceptively bucolic name, Meadow Brook. The place I recall was a backwater, and a good bit of it had been used as a dumping ground by the townspeople. My favorite pool was more like a small pond because the water was mostly stagnant; it flowed, ever so slowly, into a reedy marsh from where one of our neighbors, an adventurous scavenger and hunter named Secondo

Mola, harvested large snapping turtles (for the eggs, and the meat for soup) and muskrat (for the pelts).

However unlovely, the little pool was mine, and that's where I caught my first fish, a sunfish, on a yellow-and-green fiberglass pole that had been a birthday present from my uncle and godfather, Ralph Ortenzi, when I turned six.

I spent a lot of time around that homely pool in summer, watching turtles and frogs, and catching an occasional sunny.

I fantasized about setting up camp or building a little cabin beside the pool and keeping watch over it. I was not familiar with the term "riverkeeper" until I was 40 years old and visited Montana and, on a chilly day besides DePuy Spring Creek, smelled wood burning and stepped into a warming hut. That's when I learned that some people are actually paid to manage fisheries; it stems from the British tradition of hiring "riverkeepers" to maintain and protect trout and salmon streams.

Lines 48 and 49 from Robert Frost's "Birches" goes: "I'd like to get away from Earth awhile, And then come back to it and begin over."

Frost said he would come back as a climber and swinger of birches. I would come back as a riverkeeper on Father's Day Creek, and, in that fantasy I would have started my career at age 7 or 8, back in East Bridgewater, along little Meadow Brook.

East Bridgewater – population 8,500 when I lived there – did not offer much in the way of trout fishing.

But it provided a lot of other things: A nurturing base for growing up and a sense of the big world beyond, if only from the sound of the train coming through, blowing its whistle as it passed during the night.

Sometimes the train stopped at the Woodward & Wright Last Company – they made wooden lasts, or forms, for shoes there – and I only knew this because, on the way to school the next morning, we walked over the tracks, and there would be burned-out road flares with piles of ash next to them; workers from either the train or from Woodward & Wright had set them out the night before. I cannot say I ever saw the train come through town. But I certainly heard and saw evidence of it, and it fostered wishful thinking about the future and the notion of moving on.

Some people have it all planned by the time they arrive at senior year in high school. For others, it just happens – college or a job takes them away. Or maybe they fall in love and part of the deal involves settling somewhere else. Some people moved away from East Bridgewater in one damn hurry – a couple of my classmates were never heard from again after graduation night – and others were not so sure about leaving the hometown.

But all who grew up in East Bridgewater took a piece of that small, simple and mostly delightful place with us.

Looking back, a lot of it seems idyllic now – playing outside all day in the summer until it was dark, inventing games, walking "up town" to buy a popsicle, riding my bike through woods and across fields, pretending I was Steve McQueen on a motorcycle in "The Great Escape," going to the polo grounds for the Fourth of July bonfire. One year, when John F. Kennedy was president, the East Bridgewater Commercial Club gave JFK's rival in the Cold War a hot seat: They capped the town's annual 40-foot bonfire with an outhouse, and inside, seated on a toilet, his red Communist Party necktie flapping in the summer breeze, was an effigy of Soviet premiere Nikita Khrushchev.

We played Little League games on the old polo grounds and, at the time, there was no Mercy Rule to bring a game to an early end when one team had an insurmountable lead. The adults in East Bridgewater must have thought a good lickin' was just part of life, just what we needed, a rite of passage for eight-year-old boys. So the games would go on and on, 15-0, 26-2, 36-3. I played for the Woodard & Wright Last Co. While we appreciated the team sponsorship, we found ourselves at a distinct psychological disadvantage, having the word "Last" sewn into our jerseys. And that was where we ended up that first season.

The fall in East Bridgewater brought high school football games and the smell of burning leaves. The winters were long, snowy, rainy and gray and, for long stretches, muddy and miserable. Plymouth County had an average annual average snowfall of 37 inches, and it was not unusual to get a foot of snow overnight. But life mostly went on, we mostly went to school after a big snow. And it was the short, stout, ruddy-faced man named Eddie Kenneally who saw that we did. If there was snow overnight, you knew there was a chance the schools might be closed. But if, by 6 am or so, you heard a cowbell out front, if you heard a man barking, "H'yar," and, if you could feel the thud of big horse hooves, strong and heavy through the snow, you knew you were going to have classes that day. To confirm it, you rubbed the frost off a window so you could see Eddie Kenneally driving his huge draft horse on a sidewalk plow, his Dalmatian scampering alongside him in the snow.

As much as we appreciated a day off now and then, school was really the central part of the East Bridgewater experience – where you made friends, and where I had the good fortune of having some really great, committed teachers. When I take account of people who had the most influence on me – who took an interest in me, supported me – six of the Top Ten were teachers in the East Bridgewater public schools.

Spring meant the end of mud time, ice-out at Forge Pond, fishing for hornpout, Little League parades, trying to catch herring in a herring run with our bare hands, and failing every time.

The summer meant endless backyard baseball games and hanging out at my little piece of Meadow Brook.

I thought about the place so much – almost as much as I thought about baseball – that I took it to bed with me as I reviewed all the activities of a busy summer day. I imagined that I would construct an observatory alongside the pool. I would dig a big hole next to the brook and insert a large steel container, like an underground storage tank. My father was a foundryman, and the Santillis made castings from aluminum; certainly they would help me acquire the steel tank, outfit it with an air vent, a topside hatch door and watertight observatory window, then dig away the bank between the window and the water. From inside the tank, which I planned to line with blankets and pillows, I would be able to unravel the mysteries of the pool by regarding all of its comings and goings. My strategic plan included, eventually, charging admission for others who wanted to watch the fish, turtles, frogs and muskrat from my private observatory. However, I would reserve the right to ban any neighborhood kids who had mocked the idea, starting with the local wise guy, Stevie Abatti. No way was he getting a seat by the window.

I sketched plans in a notebook. I showed my father. I showed my older brother, a scientist still in graduate school at the time. While the reactions were encouraging, I never got the funding I needed. But the scheme has never left my mind.

There was a second place in East Bridgewater, also by a river, that I considered my own, and it was just another five-minute walk further up West Union Street, toward a place known as Cinder Hill because there used to be an ironworks with a big furnace in the area. There was a spot on the Matfield River where, in summer, I would wait in the mud to catch crayfish in a Maxwell House coffee can, and I approached my quarry with such intensity I was pretty much oblivious to the odor of sewage. To some people, it was the polluted old Matfield; to me, it looked like a pristine white-water river from a New England calendar on the wall of a barbershop. Despite the reality – foul water, devoid of fish, debased by years of industrial use and human waste – I dreamed about building an underwater observatory there, too.

I agree that the Matfield looked a lot better than it smelled. But the smell was not as acute in winter, when I trekked alone through the snow to snoop around in the woods and along the floodplain. I considered it my private scouting grounds, and my discoveries included bird nests on naked branches, rabbit tracks and what turned out to be the ruins of one of the town's 22 long-abandoned mills. The one by the Matfield, I later learned, had manufactured arms for the Revolutionary War.

When I look back on those walks in the winter woods, I have a distinct memory of the silence in them – even with West Union Street just a few hundred yards away. On a Sunday afternoon in January or February, the rush of the Matfield over rocks and under plates of ice was loud and clickety-clear, steady and even mesmerizing, the only sound for hundreds of precious minutes of my youth. Decades later, I still find myself staring into streams and listening to their chatter. I do that on Father's Day Creek when the fishing is slow.

When I arrived at the creek, there was nothing unusual to note, just the easy riffles, water running over rocks, splashing white and silver, then turning to suds, then flattening into something like black tea speckled with foamy bubbles. As I hiked along the creek, I looked for signs of life in the water. In the first hour or so, as the sun started to spill through the hemlocks, I heard nothing but the stream itself. But then, around 7 am, I heard a soft plunk 30 feet away. It was a sound distinct from that of a stick falling in the river or the sound of an all-business kingfisher dive-bombing a minnow. It was a feeding trout – after 10 years of trout fishing, a sound as familiar as my father's voice – and it was rising to one of a dozen types of flies that regularly hatch in the creek and swim to the surface. After a few seconds, there was another soft plunk, another trout rising behind the first, giving away its position. I saw small, tan bugs emerging from the water, trying to unfurl their wings before the trout ate them. And then, as the rising sun hit Father's Day Creek, there were five trout popping up in the feeding lanes to smack at

Trichoptera, the caddis fly that is probably the most abundant critter in the creek, a regular entrée on a trout's menu. My heart rose at the prospect of a morning in paradise. I prepared to make my first cast of the day.

From time to time, I would get a chance to fish in the saltwater of the New England coast, almost always with my father and my uncle. My father might have enjoyed fishing as sport, but he saw it primarily as another way of providing for his family. We fished with heavy poles, sinkers, barbed hooks and bait. We took flounder from bays, haddock and cod from the Atlantic, off Plymouth, Massachusetts. We brought home everything we caught in buckets and tubs – haddock, cod, striped bass, bluefish, mackerel and eels. Only sharks were returned to the water, and we always killed them before tossing them back. Even when I was a kid fishing in ponds, the notion of releasing anything but the tiniest fish did not enter my mind. I brought home bass, pickerel and sunfish. What was the point of catching them if you could not show them to your parents, especially your father?

But, as I grew older, my view changed. I wanted no part of fishing for food. I wanted to fix streams, not strip them. I could afford to buy trout for dinner; I did not have to kill wild ones. That's why I was careful to wet my hands and release any trout I caught in Father's Day Creek. And, elsewhere, as a journalist, I had seen what a wild trout stream can be if you just leave it alone, or, even better, actively protect it from abuse.

In 1995, I took a trip to a place called Lostland. That was the name of a forested area with a pretty little stream, Lostland Run, that dropped through a grove of rhododendron and hemlocks on its way to the

North Branch of the Potomac River in the far western reach of Maryland, at its border with West Virginia. It was a hidden beauty, in the cradle of a forested mountain range. There were wow-inducing cliffs and woods along both sides, and vistas as big and as gorgeous as what you might see in Montana or some other western state. The North Branch meandered for many miles through long tunnels of sycamore, maple and hemlock.

Lostland Run was one of several brooks that fed the North Branch.

There was a time, for a century or more, when the Potomac was part of the old frontier. It served the pioneering of the West and the early American industrial age. In the process, "the Nation's River" became one of its most polluted. The same was true of its North Branch. In the 1800s, in Garrett County, men cut down the trees, built railroads and dug deep into the ground for coal. The logging left hardly a tree standing in the county by the early 1900s. The mining was vast and deep, with honeycombs of tunnels under great hilly stretches of the region. Often the tunneling reached underground rivers. Eventually, as miners pulled coal ore out of the Earth, they left behind massive subterranean reservoirs that held millions of gallons of acidic water. When that water gushed up through the ground, into little brooks like Lostland Run, it carried a poison that threw everything out of balance and killed virtually all life in the North Branch. For decades no one bothered to fish the river; it was left for dead. The native brook trout disappeared, their cool and clean habitats ruined.

The North Branch became orange and ugly. Hunters and hikers would pass through the area, but not fishermen. As a fishery, the North Branch of the Potomac became something people referred to in the past tense.

Historians and fisheries biologists understood what had been lost when they read 18th Century accounts of "fish lying so thick with their heads above the water" and of "the Potomac River [being] without any question the most pleasant and healthful in all the country." Records show that substantial numbers of trout were harvested until the late 19th century.

But the mining expanded at a time when the words "environmental" and "regulation" never appeared in the same sentence. By the middle of the 20th Century, more than 50 surface and deep mines in Maryland and West Virginia had been abandoned, and they spilled acid into the brooks with every rain. An estimated 118,000 pounds of mine acid seeped each day into the North Branch. It was a surreal tableau – a foul river that flowed through some of the most beautiful and wild countryside in the region. At one point in the 1980s, the state had to ban the consumption of any fish in a long stretch of the North Branch because of the presence of cancer-causing dioxin. By 1987, Ken Pavol, the regional fisheries manager for the Maryland Department of Natural Resources, and Alan Klotz, a biologist, found only sunfish and suckers in the North

Branch. They wrote this in their annual report: "Until minimum water quality can be maintained on a year-round basis, fish and invertebrate faunas will continue to be sparse or nonexistent . . . No game fish introductions are warranted at this time." Why stock a dead river?

But, less than a decade later, when I visited Lostland for *The Baltimore Sun*, men and women who knew the territory – including biologists who tend to study things for years before making any pronouncements – declared the North Branch to be a river in recovery. In just a few years, the hand of man had played a therapeutic part in bringing the trout back to the licks and brooks that fed the big river below.

The North Branch had become part of what environmentalist Bill McKibben called the "new frontier" of the Eastern United States, part of a vast re-greening of the countryside. "The old frontiers have closed," McKibben declared in an essay for *The Atlantic* in 1995. "A new frontier may be opening here – an expanding frontier of recovery that, given infinite human care and nurturing, might follow the waves of destruction across the continent and then around the world."

The North Branch and Lostland Run, and rivers and licks like it, were prime to be part of this new frontier. And Father's Day Creek, with proper stewardship, could be restored to its historic best. A few years earlier, McKibben had written a seminal book, "The End of Nature," in which he argued that we had so profoundly altered our world that nature was no longer a force independent of human beings. It was a deeply disturbing thing to contemplate. "More and more frequently," McKibben wrote, "these changes will clash with our perceptions until, finally, our sense of nature as eternal and separate is washed away, and we will see all too clearly what we have done." But now, with his descriptions of the new frontier, he suggested that we had the power to fix things. Just as humans had exploited the land and poisoned the North Branch of the Potomac, they might be able to conjure up an antidote.

And they did.

While I was visiting Lostland with Ken Pavol and another natural resources official, Gary Yoder, I heard a hollow clang in the woods. The mechanical sound, strange and harsh next to the natural laughter of the cascading brook, came from a lime doser, a perpetual motion machine designed to drop pulverized limestone into the stream from a tall cylindrical hopper, something like a silo. It was one of the most unusual things I had ever seen. Water streamed into one of two steel troughs beneath the hopper. The troths were about two feet long and V-shaped. They were welded to each other and balanced on a pipe, alternately tipping to the left or right as each filled with water. Just above these tipping troths, a piston-like device appeared to punch into the bottom of the hopper, releasing a bucket's worth of powdered lime. When the troth tipped, several gallons of milky, acid-neutralizing water splashed into Lostland Run. Each clang represented another dose of lime.

"In 1980, there were no brook trout up here," Pavol told me that day. "Now they're back, some of them in little pools right up here below the doser."

Four of these magical dosers were installed in the woods of Garrett County, giving the little brooks and the big river they fed an intravenous of antacid to neutralize the foul, orange drainage from abandoned mines. Several miles downstream, the treated water entered the massive lake behind the Jennings Randolph Dam. From the outflow of the dam, the North Branch roared on for several miles. Its rehabilitation took years, but considering the duration and scope of its degradation, the patient had a relatively speedy recovery.

In 1993, the state lifted the fishing ban. Ken Pavol carried buckets of baby smallmouth bass to the river to see what would happen.

And something remarkable happened.

The bass lived. They grew. They even reproduced – the first time that had happened in the North Branch in more than a century. The smallmouth somehow adapted and learned to see through the murky waters and find crayfish, a prime food source. Pavol discovered trout several miles downstream of the dam, an indication that the water was cold enough and healthy enough to sustain the most fragile of fish. By the time Pavol retired from government service, there were rainbows reproducing over several miles of the North Branch.

The North Branch rainbows resulted from creative tinkering to restore a natural resource. Last I checked, the lime dosers were still at work in the forests of western Maryland, and fly anglers were catching healthy rainbows on float trips down the North Branch. In the summer of 2018, my son, Nick, caught one of the largest of them, about 18 inches long.

The rivers of the East, victims of human abuse for extended periods of our history, are remarkably resilient. Tinker with the ones that need tinkering, or just leave them alone long enough, and their natural inhabitants will return.

One day, on the way to the Father's Day Creek, I pulled off the highway to scout another little brook. It was so close to the highway I could not imagine fish living there. But I found the brook – and, remarkably, brook trout.

A beautiful creature, particularly in fall, when it's in the mood for love, the brookie is all green, silver, blue, with dashes of raspberry and orange – a splashy dresser in spawning season. The brookies once lived in all the little streams in the East that have been degraded since Colonial times. Settlers felled trees, farmers planted crops and, in many cases, the little waterways were rendered too warm and muddy to hold brookies.

But nature has its way, and the brookies have survived. They manage to find the cold, clean water of a few feeder streams, where they spawn and eat big meals before winter sets in.

I followed the brook to a place where it was no more than two feet wide and two feet deep – crystal clean, and the world of the fish remarkably visible.

Throngs of minnows darted about as I waded along the grassy bank. Rocks were covered with aquatic insect life. There were dozens of crayfish, three to four inches long, thrusting backward and scampering for cover beneath rocks. I poked one gently with a small stick and, like a Chesapeake blue crab on a chicken neck, he grabbed it and held on with his claws as I lifted him out of the water. He was at least 5 inches long. He would make a fine autumn feast for the huge trout that I suddenly spooked with my clumsy invasion.

Holy Shit! Did you see that?

The fish rocketed away through a 10-foot-wide pool below a sycamore tree and I never saw him again. The sight of the large trout, the flash of yellow-orange as he turned momentarily on his side, left me breathless.

There were small brown trout and a few brookies all through the stream. The roar of highway traffic never left my ears during this two-hour hike across an overgrown pasture and into woods. I could feel the vibration and displacement of air from speeding 18-wheelers. That's how close I was to the highway.

The colonists cut all the trees that formed the canopy that protected this brook. For two centuries, farmers tilled the soil, and mud washed into the brook. Livestock likely tramped through it. Construction crews built a major highway within 100 yards of it. Millions of cars and trucks spiked the air around it with pollution. The state spiced the highway with salt and chemicals during countless snow and ice storms.

And still the little brook survived, and even thrived.

I stood with my back to the manmade highway, with its mechanical grind-and-hum, and gazed into this sweet-water world filled with life, persevering, still there for me to behold. I was knee-deep in a miracle.

Before I start fishing, allow me to offer an explanation about the name of this creek. I named it Father's Day not just to cloak its identity, but because I fished it every Father's Day for 10 years – first with a spinning rod and lures, and then with a fly rod and flies. My explorations were almost always conducted in the early morning hours of a Saturday or Sunday, when my wife and I managed to get to her parents' weekend place. By this Father's Day 2000, I know the creek pretty well. I know the good spots to enter the water. I know the deep holes. I know the best places to make a long back-cast, and I rarely get my line caught in a tree or bush anymore. The first year I fished the creek, I wore rubber chest waders, big clumsy things I had purchased for surf fishing at Cape Hatteras. They were fine on a sandy beach, awful on slippery boulders and gravel in a fast-moving creek. It wasn't long – maybe 15 minutes – before I slipped and the river poured into the waders. They filled fast, and I thought I was going to drown. I tossed my spinning rod to the bank, loosened the shoulder straps and wiggled out of the waders. It was April and it was cold. I never used those damn waders again. I switched to felt-sole wading boots that provided better footing on the rocks. I also made the switch to fly fishing. Now, here I am, a decade into my explorations of Father's Day Creek, confident in my wading and my casting, and yet still worried that too many of the bait-fishers had caught and killed too many of the wild trout. But something special and unexpected happened. Epiphany is a good word for it. If there's one place I have witnessed the healing powers of the divine – the work of the same Great Spirit to whom the native Delawares once paid respects – it was in the second coming of the trout in Father's Day Creek. For me, the resurrection became official on this third Sunday of June 2000, when so many trout at once started rising to caddisflies, and I stepped into the water.

One day in the 1990s, I joined my friend Mike Flanagan, by then retired from his Major League pitching career, for a hike along a creek in a secluded stretch of woods and farmland behind the 19th Century Maryland farmhouse he and his wife had purchased a few months earlier. This was a place on private land that had been left alone. No one had fished it in years. At least that's what the neighboring landowners had told Mike.

During the hike, I spotted something white on the dark creek bed from 30 feet away. I have a keen eye for trash in pretty places – not the big, obvious chunks of man-made debris that appear along riverbanks, or the bright blue plastic bags that blossom in trees, but the minutiae of trash. I can easily spot the smallest souvenirs of American society – flattened beer cans, pieces of plastic from toys, stove bolts, roofing nails, fishhooks – that end up in the pretty places where trout live.

I assumed what I saw that day was a plastic foam cup.

But it wasn't, and there's a story in what it turned out to be.

As Mike and I hiked deeper into the place, a mile or more from paved roads, and no houses in sight, it became apparent that Mike's neighbors probably had it right: No other human being had visited the place recently, and maybe not in a long time. That is not something you can know for sure, but it is something you can sense. We both got the impression – and it wasn't just wishful thinking – that no one had fished the stream in a long time.

From a distance, which is how most people see the creek, assuming they see it at all, it was not alluring to people who fish. It appeared to have been battered by years of erosion from upstream farming; the bottom was sandy and silty, only gravelly near its riffles. The water flow was moderate to slow. It was hard to imagine trout living in such a place. It looked like another lost cause from the old frontier.

One thing I've learned from the delight of fishing for browns, rainbows and brookies – they all prefer pretty places, where the water is clear, clean and cold. They could not exist otherwise. They can swim among sneakers and old tires, they can forage for invertebrate lunch in river bottoms littered with beer cans. But they cannot live where the water gets too warm and polluted.

In the eastern United States, wild trout live in freestone streams fed by cold springs or in tailwaters downstream of dams. A healthy canopy of trees helps, too. "Trout are the canaries in the coal mine," a conservationist and fly angler told me. "You can judge the health of a stream, the quality of the water, by whether wild trout can live and breed in it."

Mike and I went out to look for canaries. We took our fly rods.

It was a warm day in the woods for Mike's first survey of the stream. We kept walking and wading, going upstream, sampling wild watercress along the way. We hoped for something we dared not express – that the stream might be cold enough and clean enough to hold trout.

Up close, the creek looked better than we had thought. In places, the water was only six inches deep, but in pockets, along the banks, under the roots of leaning sycamores, it was three and sometimes four feet deep. There were a couple of long pools that looked fishy. The water was clear. I dropped a stainless steel stream thermometer to the bottom and let it sit there for a few minutes. When I saw the results – 54 degrees Fahrenheit – I practically shouted the good news. At the end of one of the driest summers in Maryland history, the stream had a steady flow and a temperature suitable for a trout habitat.

We continued walking and wading. We started spotting small, easily spooked fish. I thought they might be creek chubs, an annoying, oversized minnow that can withstand high water temperatures and get between a fly angler and trout. We saw what I thought was a crowd of silvery chubs in about two feet of water under the exposed roots of a sycamore. I got on my knees and cast a wet fly, a nymph imitation, below the tree and immediately had a hook-up. When the fish turned out to be a baby brown trout, about six inches long, Mike and I got excited. I don't remember exactly what we said to each other – "Holy shit!" might have been involved – but it was as if we had just discovered gold.

We quickly returned the little fish to the water.

The creek turned hard to the north, then hard to the east. I saw a trout sip at a bug on the surface of the stream, just below another large, leaning sycamore. So did Mike. He cast a mayfly imitation to it. A brown trout poked its nose up and took the fly, and we were both surprised at the fish's vigor. It was 14 inches long and fat, colorful and muscular. We took a good look, then slipped it back into the stream. We were too excited to speak.

We had found trout where we had not expected to find any fish at all.

We felt as though we had discovered the place.

Certainly, once upon a time, when there were no farms, when all around the creek was forest, native people had come here and fished. Or maybe the farmers who settled on the land fished the stream and took trout. Maybe, years later, a wealthy landowner had stocked these waters with brown trout, and now their descendants lived there.

It was just upstream from where we had landed the 14-inch brown that I saw something white in the water. At first, I assumed it was trash – a wad of paper, or more likely a foam cup. It was one of the few pieces of trash I'd seen in this pretty place.

But as I approached, I realized the white was not trash from humans, but something from the stream itself.

I yelled for Mike, then pulled up my sleeves, reached into the cold water and raised the grapefruit-size head of what had been a four- or five-pound trout. It was spotted, brown, green and yellow. The white that had caught my eye was the underside of the long, gnarled jaw.

The head filled my hand. One of the trout's eyes had been poked out. The head appeared to have been ripped away from the body, which we figured to have been at least two feet long. A heron or osprey, both of which frequent the area, must have found Bubba before we did.

Mike and I were awed by the size of the trout and humbled by the thought of a bird catching it. We felt privileged, that autumn afternoon, to have discovered a creek in suburban-rural Maryland that, decades after its degradation, could still provide kingdom to such a large, regal fish.

Alerted to the rising trout in Father's Day Creek, I clipped the Adams parachute from my tippet and tied on a tan caddis imitation, made from deer hair. My first few casts did not impress the trout in the feeding lanes. But soon I got the fly to the right spot, where the drift was perfect, and pow! . . . A frisky little brown trout, about 10 inches long, took it. He swam away from me, and as the line tightened, he jumped out of the water. I landed him with my net, and returned him quickly to the stream. The commotion did not spook the other trout in the pool; they kept feeding. In the next 10 minutes, I caught two more, each about a foot long. This was already an unusually good day, and so I savored the moment by sitting on a boulder and reflecting on what had just happened – and what used to happen in that same spot: Nothing. In those first years of fishing on Father's Day, it was clear that the creek's wild trout population had been depleted, most likely by the bait anglers. There was no other explanation for it. The water was clean and cold, and there was plenty of insect life. A few times a year,

I made some casts to spots in Father's Day Creek where experience told me I should have found a feeding trout. I found very few, and none more than 6 inches. I felt guilty stressing such small fish, so I decided to leave the river alone. I visited every summer and fall, mainly to have a look around. Once the Pennsylvania deer hunting season ended and it was safe to hike through the woods, I checked on the creek as the snow started to fall. I returned each spring. There were impressive afternoon hatches of caddis, the aquatic insects whose emergence from a stream should incite a riot of surface feeding. But rarely was there a ring left by a rising trout. So I came to see the little stream as a lost opportunity – perfect conditions for trout, but no protection from its main predator, Piscatores hominum. The river should have had a no-harvest rule, but it suffered from this oversight, and men came back each year and took what they wanted, just as their fathers and grandfathers had done. Instead of singing the splendors of nature, Father's Day Creek howled of the greed of man. But then, unexpectedly, something significant happened in 1994. The state suddenly stopped stocking the creek, and the hunter-gatherers lost interest in the place and turned away, like football fans from a concession that runs out of hot dogs. Within a few years, the fishing started to improve. Those brown trout I caught in the first hour of Father's Day 2000 had been born in the stream, and they had been given a chance to live and thrive. I sat on the boulder and gave thanks for that.

For $35, I joined Trout Unlimited – a national conservation group, not a fishing club. I still enjoyed fishing, especially when it took me to pretty places with a fly rod and good friends, but I became more interested in protecting cold-water fisheries. Fly fishing for trout helped me understand, in a very real way, how connected everything is.

Baltimore sits on the upper reaches of the Chesapeake Bay, the nation's largest estuary. I would often fish to the north, in Pennsylvania, in the small creeks and streams that feed the big rivers that eventually flow to the bay. The Chesapeake has been in a life-or-death struggle for as long as I have lived in Maryland, more than 40 years, following decades of pollution from heavy industry, municipal sewage and stormwater systems, and agricultural runoff. Some years the prognosis for the bay's health is terrible. Sometimes it starts to look promising. Surprising numbers of people pay attention to the bay's health; they are conversant in the issues because the Chesapeake makes news a lot, and thousands of Marylanders and Virginians still earn their livings from it. I have not commissioned a survey to prove it, but my guess is that people who live in the Chesapeake region are more actively conscious of environmental issues than are the inhabitants of other huge swaths of the country.

You would think that would mean public consensus, and that consensus would have saved the bay by now. The problem is ever-escalating human pressure

– from agriculture and from population growth – along all the rivers that lead to it.

Some years ago, my family went hiking through what's known as the Grand Canyon of Pennsylvania, Pine Creek Gorge, about 200 miles north of Baltimore. I wanted to fish in Pine Creek and so I put on my waders, stepped into the stream and walked over rocks until I was in water above my waist, about four feet deep. Amazingly, I could still see my wading boots. The water quality was exquisite, a paradise for trout.

Where the Chesapeake begins, up in the mountain springs and licks that feed the creeks that feed the big rivers, the water runs clear and cold enough that trout can survive. But as the water flows down through the Susquehanna, the Potomac, the Patapsco and the Patuxent, it gathers nitrogen-rich runoff from farmland and suburban lawns. It absorbs the massive drainage of an urbanized population.

Where my wife, son and daughter hiked, you could put your hand into a feeder spring in a cool, mossy place in the woods and feel the birth water of the bay run cold and fresh over your hands. And then you could stand back, your head in the low-hanging hemlocks, and watch the water splash down through the damp, forested mountainside on its way to Pine Creek, deep in the gorge below, and from there more than 40 miles to the West Branch of the Susquehanna, and from there to the big river, which provides the Chesapeake with half of its fresh water.

Imagine this: One hundred years ago, a visitor to Pine Creek Gorge would have found nothing but mud in his hands. By then, men had stripped the whole range bare, sending the lumber to growing East Coast markets and to the shipbuilders in Baltimore. The rivers were poisoned with tannery waste and mine acid. The mountainous lands that today attract tourists were once known as the Pennsylvania Desert.

It would have been hard to stand there and watch a mudslide in 1909 and imagine that such a place could ever recover.

But some people did imagine it; they insisted on it. So there is a massive swath of green in north-central Pennsylvania today, tens of thousands of acres reforested, on the way back to its preindustrial best, part of Bill McKibben's new frontier.

Of course, leaving lands alone to become green again is easy compared to Chesapeake recovery. A century ago, there were only about 3 million people living in the watershed; there are 18 million today, and all of us have to eat, all of us flush toilets and most of us still rely on energy from fossil fuels. The population is expected to reach 20 million in the next decade. It's hard to imagine the Chesapeake getting better as the region becomes more congested.

But I remain an optimist. If the rest of us do our part and demand sustained commitment to the Chesapeake by the politicians we elect and the businesses we support, the bay might one day stop wheezing and coughing. I believe we can save a resource and live in better balance with it.

When I go fishing in Pine Creek or in Father's Day Creek, or wherever the fly rod takes me, I try to look downstream and imagine the Chesapeake Bay in full recovery: blue crabs plentiful and heavy, the waters safe for swimming, bay grasses expanding, dead zones contracting, and my wading boots visible in four feet of Baltimore Harbor.

Because he was a chef and because he liked to make everyone laugh, I knew what my father-in-law would say today when I return to the house from fishing: "Hey, Rodricks, where's the fish?" He might even greet me in the driveway with a cast-iron frying pan and ask if I caught enough trout for a Father's Day feast. He knew the answer: No fish today, no fish any day. People often ask me if I eat the trout I catch, and I say no, every time. In fact, I have no memory of the last wild trout I kept for the table. I was an easy convert to the catch-and-release idea: Fool fish with flies tied on barbless hooks that almost never draw blood, land the fish, then gently release them; they'll be bigger when you catch them next year. It's what I teach my son and my daughter. They might one day see even this as a cruel invasion of the natural world. They might come to see my kind of fishing the way I came to see my father's, and they might not want to fish at all. But that will be their choice, not mine. As long as I can fish, I fish. I fish and I catch. I catch and I release. Especially on Father's Day Creek. Enough of sitting and reflecting. Time to find another spot and start casting.

The first time I saw the stretch above the gorge, I am pretty sure my heart picked up a beat or two. Anyone who fishes with flies and understands the habits of trout would appreciate the vista: On the left, a forested hillside, thick with rhododendron and dabs of mountain laurel. On the right, hemlock trees. And in the middle, a stream 50 feet wide, with riffles and long pools, deep pockets behind scattered boulders and a few fallen trees – all sorts of shaded places for trout to hold. "It looks fishy," is what a trout angler would say. But that's really a demeaning understatement. Plenty of places "look fishy." The creek above the gorge is a trout paradise.

The first time I saw it, on Father's Day 1995, I felt as though I had discovered a passageway to a hidden treasure room and I immediately looked around to see if anyone else had noticed. I looked for signs of other humans, and there were few: A broken board from an old fence, a plastic jug, a length of metal chain, a few pieces of porcelain. Judging from the amount of debris – branches and trunks of trees, mounds of dead grass lodged in the lower limbs of trees – it was clear the creek had roared during big storms or with the snowmelt in late winter and early spring.

On my first day above the gorge, the water depth across the full width of the stream seemed to be just right for trout, providing plenty of places for them to feed, and the water temperature was in the high 50s, close to ideal. We all have our ideas about perfection: Baseball says it's when a pitcher goes nine innings and does not allow a single batter to reach base. In ten-pin bowling, 10 strikes in 10 frames constitute perfection. In high school, it's acing a science exam. But those are all objective measurements of the perfect. It's the subjective – our personal visions of the ideal, based on our experiences, our biases, our emotional chemistry – that mark us as individuals. My son and daughter were both good ice hockey players, but they seemed perfect to me when they made a generous and accurate pass of the puck to a teammate. My father-in-law, a French-American chef, could grill a New York strip steak to perfection, and I still picture him holding a finished one on a serving fork, looking for a taker at a Fourth of July picnic. When he stood before it in Florence, my older brother declared Michelangelo's David so perfect it made him weep. Tears were reported among audience members at the conclusion of the world premiere of Mahler's 9th Symphony. I understand weeping at the perfect. When you see or hear something incredible – something as constant as time or something magnificent for just a moment – it can reach a deep place. It can sear the soul. It inspires. It gives hope. It makes you feel part of the once and future world. And so I believe I approached perfection when I first waded into Father's Day Creek above the gorge on that bright Sunday morning in 1995. A section of river never looked so ideal to me, so pristine, a solemn and bright place. I had that special sense of being the first man to ever see it, and I felt immediately protective of it. I envied the fish that lived behind its boulders, and, of course, I wanted to try and catch them. I wanted to meet them.

Perhaps it's a flaw in my thinking – that I should disturb such a paradise by trying to hook its inhabitants, or "rip some lips," as Mike Flanagan used to say. But I concede that soft vice. I find the challenge irresistible, and the curiosity to see the trout who live in the creek takes me back to boyhood, when I wanted to build that observation room by the skanky river near my house.

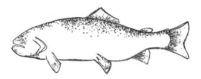

In the second hour of fishing on Father's Day, I hiked up to a spot in the gorge section and swung the same caddis fly downstream, to an eddy at the bottom of a large pool. The drift was long and fast, and I never lost sight of the fly. Another brown trout, this one longer and fatter than the first three, took it and jumped twice before I landed him. I was excited by the trout's size and energy. Nearby, I spotted a boulder covered with the dried shucks of large stone flies. This trout had had plenty of insects to feed on, and he had the best seat in the house – just outside of the fast current, against a pile of rocks and sticks at the end of a pool. On June 18, 2000, I was convinced that Father's Day Creek was in full revival, and the reason was written on a sign posted on a tree near the road by the bridge where I had parked my car: "These waters not stocked. Catch and release encouraged." The sign had first appeared in 1994. I was surprised and happy to see it, though skeptical about what good it might do. Apparently, the landowners had complained about the behavior of the spring fishermen who hiked through their woods to the river. The commonwealth had decided to stop stocking my favorite section of Father's Day Creek. And when word of this got around, the hunter-gatherers took their appetites elsewhere. Pierre said, "There's no trout there anymore," and he went off to harvest stocked fish from some other Pennsylvania creek. The sign meant the wild brown trout would likely be left alone. I suddenly felt, even in the height of spring, and even in the years when I got skunked, that I was the only person on Father's Day Creek. I might have been the only man who still believed in it, too. I had a sense that it could make a comeback from the purging of the wild browns, but kept my expectations in check. Turns out, I had been given the privilege of watching a beautiful thing: What happens when people leave a natural trout stream alone.

I think of my father when I fish, no matter where I am, because the best times I had with him involved fishing. Joe Rodricks was 40 when I was born, 42 when my brother Eddie was born, and while we knew him as a strong guy – Iron Joe – his work had broken his back. Being a foundryman caused him spinal problems that led to several surgeries, and I have a distant memory of him sitting in our dining room in traction. He had a device that involved weights and a pulley that fit over a door. He sat in a chair with his chin in a cloth halter, and the weights relieved pressure on what I assume were compressed vertebrae.

I think it's accurate to say that he was physically worn down by the time my brother and I were running around in the backyard. He was a good 10-pin bowler – according to the engraving on a trophy, he had the high single for his league one year – but he could not throw a baseball overhand. So you won't find in any scrapbook a classic photograph of father and sons playing catch. His physical limitations – the arched and aching back, his fatigue, and later his emphysema – made him seem a lot older than fathers of my friends and classmates.

We did not go camping. He did not take us kayaking. He did not teach us tennis. He had little money for vacations. The lack of physical activity together diminished the opportunity for father-son bonding. I don't mean that as a criticism, just an observation, and as a way to offer advice: If you are able to join your son or daughter in physical recreation – something as simple as a bicycle trip or a hike in the woods, or a little fishing – do it, and do it often. Americans have so much leisure time now, compared to what my parents' generation had, it's a shame to squander all of it on yourself.

And talk.

Talk to your kids, especially during the early years. Show them stuff – how to fix a flat tire, how to care for tomato plants, how to cook pancakes. Explain things. Kids are curious, and fathers should not hold back when asked questions. Get close to your kids when they're young, and they might talk to you when they're teenagers. You might be able to have civil, adult conversations instead of what I had – incessantly testy exchanges that led to foolish and sometimes violent arguments that led to a lifetime of bad feelings.

I had a chip on my shoulder when I was a teenager, and I don't know how it got there. It probably just grew there during adolescence. I was particularly cocky around my father. By the time I was in high school, my grades were decent and I was involved in sports and the student newspaper. And so I considered myself smarter and more sophisticated than Iron Joe, and certainly more athletic.

My mother undoubtedly contributed to my view of him as inferior. She constantly and openly criticized her husband for having walked away in 1968 from the foundry business he had established with his associates in 1948. That decision, which my father made for reasons of physical and mental health, resulted in a lot less income for the family, and more of a financial struggle. Those years were hard. My parents argued all the time, especially about money, and my father took after me with his temper and his iron hands for what seemed like nonsense. He was full of anger and, though hampered by physical limitations, he posed a physical threat.

Some time in high school, I became sufficiently self-aware of the chip on my shoulder when around him, so I removed it. It was a moment of sudden grow-up, a real, guilt-soaked revelation about my many contributions to the miserable nature of our relationship.

Still, he lashed out. Minor things – things I can no longer remember – set him off. In my senior year, as I turned 18, I discussed leaving home and moving in with my sister and her family near Boston.

I did not do that. I stuck it out.

I went away to college and only lived at home for brief periods after that, so there were fewer conflicts. When I came home with a full beard at the age of 22, Iron Joe looked as if he was going to slug me – one of his menacing stares – then gave me the silent treatment. One summer evening, a comment about the volume on a radio led to a physical entanglement. He got his hands around my neck and shoulders, and I squeezed his biceps and pushed him away. My girlfriend was shocked and screamed at the two of us; she had never seen anything like that in her family.

I immediately left for my sister's house and avoided visiting my parents for the rest of the year.

After I took a job with the *Baltimore Evening Sun*, I made about three annual trips to visit my mother and father in Massachusetts. But it never felt completely right. I could not shake memories of my father's anger, and I continued to worry about it. I could not shake the fear he instilled when I was a little kid. Other people told me that my father was proud of me, and I believed them. I believed he told them that. But what I sensed was rationed pride tainted by jealousy and resentments – that his father had died when he was 14; that he had never gotten to finish school; that his widowed mother had married into another family with six kids; that his physical ailments had kept him from serving in World War II and from talking about war experiences, as other men his age could; that he had not always been able to support his family; that his business had burned to the ground; that his business partner had humiliated him in front of customers; that his wife had frequently criticized his decision to leave the business just a few years after it had been rebuilt.

Instead of taking pride that he had been able to give his kids a good start toward lives better than the one he had had, he simmered in resentments and jealousy. That's my hypothesis, and it's a reflection I shared with my siblings and my psychiatrist. Maybe it's not the kindest assessment, but it's honest.

As the years went by, and I thought about the list of setbacks and challenges my father faced in life, I better understood his anger. But he never seemed to get full control of it, and the tension between us continued up until I was 32 years old. By then, the chip was long gone from my shoulder, and, when I visited them for Easter 1986, I had no intention of starting any trouble at my parents' home. That was the last thing I needed, having come out of a year of disabling depression in Baltimore, something I had kept from my parents; they knew nothing about it.

One day during the Easter visit, I stood in the kitchen, speaking quietly on the only phone in the house. The person on the other end was an aunt – my mother's youngest sister – who suffered severely from depression. We were comparing notes. I was gravely concerned about her. Everyone was. I spoke in a low tone, but my father overheard me and, while I was still on the phone with Aunt Sadie, he made some crack about "Doctor Dan" and what he apparently heard as my claim to expertise. Of course, I claimed no such thing, but I had had a terrible time during the previous year and learned a great deal about depression from a doctor I visited each week for several months. My father had no clue about any of that. But he apparently resented my display of empathy for Aunt Sadie. It was a throwback to the kind of sarcastic, deflating cracks he had made while I was growing up in that house. When I got off the phone, I snapped back at him, and that led to another explosion. Afterwards,

I felt like a foolish teenager again, and I wept. I wept because, by the spring of 1986 – when he was 72 and I was 32 – I was convinced we would never get this right.

Instead of disrupting the holiday, I decided to spend it at my sister's house.

That was the last I saw of my father until the summer, when I visited him in the intensive care unit of Brockton Hospital. He had had trouble breathing, and my sister suggested I should fly home to see him. I did. In an ICU bed, he had tubes up his nose, he could hardly speak, and there were tears in his eyes. He looked frightened. But I left that day thinking Iron Joe was going to recover, as he always did. Instead, he died a day after my return flight to Baltimore.

I was jarred by his death, and overcome with days and months of sadness fueled by guilt and regrets. We never settled our differences. We never had a heart-to-heart. We never had peace talks. Never once. It seemed too hard to even proffer the idea. And so we never found father-son equilibrium.

Had he lived longer, maybe we would have. It is hard to say. I think about all this when I go fishing.

When you are young and mainly focused on yourself – an adolescent condition – it is hard to see and appreciate the reasons people behave as they do. My father's anger was a mystery to me. It frightened and embarassed me. His rage seemed so unreasonable and unchecked, and it took several years for me to piece together and consider his life's story before

I could muster a more sympathetic view of him. By then, it was too late.

So allow me to pass along some advice, which is the whole reason I have finally committed these remembrances to this memoir: If you're in a relationship like this, either with your father or with your son, do something about it. Talk. Get into counseling. Work it out. Do not let bad feelings fester. If it's hard to break through the wall of tension, buck up and break through it. Be the one who asks for a talk. Be the one who wants to make peace. Go fishing together.

It will be hard. It will probably be painful. But, trust me on this, not as painful as the regret of never having tried.

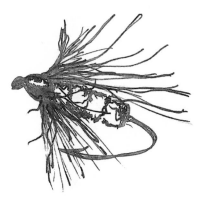

– 7:50 am

*Now I hiked above the gorge section of
Father's Day Creek to a spot where the tree
canopy opens and sunlight pours in. I stood
there for a while, downstream of a sprawling
riffle and off to the left, so that my right arm
was over the middle of the river, free of the
hemlock trees and bushes that might suddenly
reach out and snag my back-cast. I waited a
while, hoping that a trout would sip a small
fly off the surface, among the bubbles from the
riffle, and give away his position. Then I again
heard that distinct plunk-splash. It came from
the bubble line. That was my cue to cast the
caddis fly, to try and raise from these open
waters the beautiful, little brookies that live
there. By Father's Day 2000, my fishing was
more census than anything else. I wanted to
know – needed to know – if the trout were in
residence. And a fly rod was a good tool for
that job. I caught three small brook trout,
each about 10 inches long, on the same caddis
fly, and found myself, again, stopping to give
thanks and praise. I could drive back to my
in-laws' home a happy fellow. It was getting
to be 8 am. I decided to keep fishing.*

From the fishing grounds of my youth, there's a story about the exploitation of an abundant resource, the loss of it, and a long, slow recovery from oblivion. We start, as any good fishing trip does, with breakfast – in Massachusetts more than 50 years ago.

Ordering a meal in a diner might seem like the most ordinary thing but when I look back on fishing trips with my father, which often included a pre-dawn stop for breakfast, I realize how rare and special those occasions were. We really did not have that much time together, just the two of us. My father was home every night, but he was tired from the foundry work; being in his presence, while he dozed on the couch, was hardly what you would call "quality time." I looked it up: In 1965, American fathers spent an average of 2.5 hours per week with their kids; mothers spent 10 hours. So, 50 years later, when I regard the big clock of life, the time spent with Iron Joe was really just a slice, a matter of minutes, and I guess that's why the ordinary seems almost magical now.

Deep-sea fishing trips were part of my initiation into the world of men, my first peak at my father's all-male environment, where he spent most of his days and, if you follow the big clock, most of his life.

Once or twice a year, Iron Joe announced we would go fishing out of Plymouth, Massachusetts aboard the *Nan-Sue*, a 40-foot charter boat captained by a middle-aged man with tanned, weathered skin, crow's feet at his eyes and a cigarette somewhere between his fingers and lips. Every time I saw him, Joe

Perry was wearing canvas boat shoes, khakis, a brown shirt, sunglasses and a baseball cap. I was told his last name had been Americanized from the Portuguese surname Pereira, just as Rodricks had been changed from Rodrigues by some school official – most likely one of British Protestant ancestry – when my father was a kid. Such name changes were common in southeastern Massachusetts among Portuguese immigrants from Madeira Island and the Azores. So I assume shared ethnicity was the reason my father fished with no other captain in Plymouth. Fishing the deep sea was, of course, in the Portuguese DNA. Joe Perry was good at finding fish.

The exciting announcement that we were going out on the Nan-Sue triggered a ritual: My father bought canned sodas and a jar of pickled eggs for our lunch. My mother fried green peppers and made peppers-and-eggs sandwiches. I went to bed at 8 pm to rise at 4 am so we could stop to eat on the way to Plymouth. We drove in the darkness through three towns until we arrived at the only establishment with lights on at that hour – a diner on a triangular lot where two roads merged into one. It was already busy when we arrived, and the place smelled of coffee, bacon and maple syrup. The only women in the place were waitresses in white-and-blue uniforms serving coffee and big breakfasts on oval plates to men headed for work or, in our case, a day of fishing. The counter was shoulder-to-shoulder with men eating silently, or others engrossed in conversation about the Red Sox or the weather. Some of them sipped coffee and read the *Boston Record-American*, a daily Hearst tabloid that cost 10 cents a copy at the time. What a treat this was: I could order anything I wanted – eggs, pancakes, French toast, sausage, juice – and scan the sports section of the *Record*. We so seldom ate in restaurants that a $4 breakfast seemed like a feast. And it was just me and my father, which made it special, if a little strange. We had to get back on the road to Plymouth, so the focus was on eating, not talking. Still, that time with him, in the early-morning man's world, was all new and exciting. Iron Joe seemed relaxed, even happy, very different from how he was at home. He talked to me about baseball – Ted Williams, Johnny Pesky, Rudy York and Dom DiMaggio of the old Red Sox – and about what the day ahead might bring.

My father parked his Chrysler Newport at the town wharf just before sunrise. We carried an old, galvanized tub packed with our lunch, drinks and jackets to the boat. The *Nan-Sue's* diesel engines were running and gurgling when we stepped into it from the dock, and as soon as the full party was aboard, about 16 people, the boat got underway, with Perry at the helm. He took the boat out of Plymouth Harbor and headed toward the rising sun, almost due east, and then to the northeast. He looked at that moment like the perfect man – master and commander, all business, confident and comfortable with his responsibilities, two hands on the wheel, eyes on the horizon.

The ride to the fishing grounds, in what I later understood to be the Stellwagen Bank, took about two hours. The boat ran strong and straight, until the shoreline behind us disappeared, and soon we were in international waters, nothing but ocean and clouds. Sometimes humpback whales broke the surface and passengers on the boat stood up excitedly to see them. On some trips, Perry would turn up the volume on his radio so we could hear the chatter of large commercial fishing trawlers, and the chatter was often in Russian. In those days, there was a battle brewing over foreign vessels coming too close to the U.S. shoreline, with factory ships from the Soviet Union and Japan stripping away tons of seafood. Perry would stand at the wheel and shout over the engines to his attentive passengers a warning about the need to start conserving the cod and haddock of the Stellwagen. The place, he said, was being overfished by commercial vessels from other countries. Looking back now, that might have been the first time I heard someone express a need to protect a natural resource.

Once a year, my father and Uncle Ralph, one of his partners in the foundry, would treat their employees to a day of deep-sea fishing with Perry. I made a couple of those trips: a 10-year-old boy surrounded by rugged men who spent most of their days in a hot and dimly-lit foundry, fabricating gears and machine parts from cast iron. On Perry's boat, they sat in sunshine, the wind and salt in their faces. Their joking, beery banter went on all day, and sometimes one of them dropped an F bomb, and others, usually an older man, would scold the offender for his language while a kid was on deck. It was on Perry's boat during the all-male foundry outing that I first heard the word.

We sat on stools, either port or starboard, and some customers fished off the stern. I sat next to my father. We fished with fiberglass bay poles, maybe six feet long. The mate handed out bait, a slimy pile of fleshy razor clams in a cardboard tray. Our rigs included heavy bank sinkers that tugged at the tip of the rod. We dropped our lines 100 feet or more – sometimes we fished as deep as 160 feet – and waited for the cod and haddock to come along.

Perry was a serious man who was eager for his customers to catch fish for the table, particularly cod and haddock. He was patient with kids and seemed to enjoy coaching us. He showed me, and later my younger brother, Eddie, how to let the sinker hit bottom then reel up about six inches, so that the bait appeared to be floating. If the sea was choppy or the wake of another boat rocked us, the sinker bounced off the bottom, creating the sensation of a strike. It took a while to know when a cod or haddock had been hooked – to recognize that feeling from 150 feet above the feeding ground – but when I did, I never forgot it.

My father might never have been so happy as when his son hooked a fish on the *Nan-Sue*. He smiled and laughed and encouraged me as I reeled the catch to the side of the boat. "Don't stop," he'd say. "Keep it comin'." I offered the same pep talk when, late one day, he hooked a large fish and struggled to haul it up. After an initial fight, when you can feel a deep-water fish pulling at your line, it becomes dead weight as you reel it to the surface. Iron Joe had strong hands and arms, but this particular fish required every bit of upper-body muscle. Perry, impressed at my father's labors with the reel, picked up a gaff, a five-foot pole with a large hook at the end, and waited for the fish to surface. "Oh my God," somebody said. Perry leaned over the side, struck the fish with the gaff. "Cod!" he barked. He pulled it over the gunwale with a groan, and proclaimed my father the likely winner of the betting pool for the day's largest fish – and only minutes before the 4 pm cutoff. Perry weighed the cod at 36 pounds. It was between three and four feet long, a rare catch in those days. I had never seen such a large fish. I had never seen my father, or Joe Perry, so excited.

We kept almost everything we caught, and in those days mature haddock and cod were plentiful. We also caught hideous conger eels that wriggled monstrously as we brought them to the surface. Perry, or his mate, clubbed them dead and tossed them in our bucket. We had a neighbor who considered conger eel a delicacy and asked that we bring one or two home.

From his vantage at the wheel, Perry could tell instantly if you had hooked a fish – and what type it was – by watching the action on the pole as you reeled up 150 feet of line. "Looks like you got a sand shark," he'd say with a mild groan. Sand sharks were a nuisance because, once hooked, they swam in a wide circle and tangled three or four lines on the way to the surface. Perry, or his mate, dealt methodically and patiently with the tangles, sometimes from both sides of the boat at once, and they killed the sharks with their bare hands, removing the hook, then pushing hard against the shark's snout until its spine cracked. The captain and his mate tossed the dead sharks into the water, where they slowly sank and disappeared. Keep in mind, these were not large sharks. I cannot recall seeing one on Perry's boat more than four feet long, and most were just two to three feet. The routine killing of the sharks was the only thing I ever questioned – and I did so silently – about the Joe Perry-Iron Joe deep-sea fishing experience. To the captain and his mate, the sharks were a nuisance, a "trash fish" that no one was interested in eating, predators who fouled up the business of the boat. Catching cod or haddock did not bother me; I understood we were fishing for our dinner, and hopefully for multiple dinners. But it seemed cruel to remove the hook from a three-foot sand shark, then kill it because it had tangled lines and annoyed the skipper. The sight of those mortally injured sharks, some of them twitching and struggling to swim as they sank, made me sad. That might have been the first time I ever felt guilt about catching a fish.

After eight hours, our arms and hands were tired from holding the heavy poles and reeling up fish. When the boat turned for home, Perry's mate set up a wooden fish-cleaning table at the stern, pulled a filet knife from his belt, gutted each customer's catch and hurled the pink-and-gray waste into the Nan-Sue's wake. Raucous throngs of seagulls followed the boat back to Plymouth Harbor, the birds diving frantically for the entrails and swallowing them in aggressive gulps.

On some of the Nan-Sue's return trips, Perry spotted massive schools of Atlantic mackerel. When this happened, he quickly idled the boat and let it drift and yelled for us to cast our lines, with no bait on the hooks, just below the surface. Foot-long mackerel, greenish-blue with silvery gills and jaws, hit the bare hooks on each cast. The whole boat came alive, with everyone catching fish at the same time, hauling them over the gunwales, grabbing them and removing the hooks as fast as possible, and casting again. We caught them until our buckets were full, and sometimes that only took minutes.

There was such an abundance of fish in those days that Perry's warnings about a need for limits on commercial fishing probably seemed to some exaggerated. But he knew what was coming. Within a decade, the storied New England fishery was considered near collapse. Congress moved the U.S. fishing limit from 12 miles to 200 miles offshore and it established eight regional fisheries management councils around the country.

Years later, after I had gone off to college and then to Baltimore, my father reported the depressing news that the haddock and most of the cod were gone from the areas we had fished aboard the *Nan-Sue*. Perry and other captains had either retired or gone out of business. By the 1980s, when we paid someone to take us out of Plymouth on a boat, it was to watch whales with tourists. Today, the Stellwagen Bank is a national marine sanctuary. It is still open to recreational fishing and regulated commercial fishing. The New England Fishery Management Council no longer considers haddock to be overfished, but the council still views the cod stocks to be in need of protection and rebuilding.

There's this thing, an American conceit, about how you can't go home again, taken from the Thomas Wolfe novel. It took me a good while to get its full meaning. It lies somewhere between the idea that the farther you get away from a place, in time and distance, the better it looks, and the idea that we just can't face change in places that we think of as eternal. As I came back to Massachusetts for visits over the years, there were changes that saddened me – the conversion of the Plymouth deep-sea charters into whale-watch cruises was one of them. I wanted things to stay as I had remembered them. Friends, classmates and relatives died, and there was that realization, as time went by, that most things can never be as good as the first time you experienced them. But we are each blessed with both the gifts and what Garcia Marquez called the torments of memory – things great, things small, things happy, things sad, things ordinary and extraordinary – and all of it gets into our bones and becomes part of us, no matter where you end up.

I have not been deep-sea fishing since I was a teenager. I doubt I will ever do that kind of fishing again, though I often think about the *Nan-Sue* days because, starting with breakfast, they were the happiest days I ever had with my father. On the big clock of life, the *Nan-Sue* days are just a tiny slice, and more than 50 years back, but I hold them golden. I savor the memories, even dwell on them, in the hopes of erasing the rough times my father and I had later, as we grew apart. I had a dream once about bright sun and wide ocean, about being high on the flying bridge of a wooden boat like the *Nan-Sue*, moving at high speed, with Joe Perry and Iron Joe on the deck below me, and we were all on watch for feeding birds and schools of fish breaking the surface, and we were somewhere far, far beyond Plymouth, somewhere, I like to believe, across the Atlantic, off sunny Madeira.

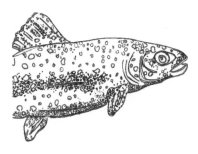

I hooked two more brown trout, each about a foot long. I found them behind boulders in the long stretch above the Father's Day Creek gorge. The take on each cast was splashy and strong. I had switched to an Adams parachute fly and was very pleased with myself when the switch proved successful. I was having a banner day because, after years of fretting about it, Father's Day Creek finally seemed to have become the trout stream I knew it could be and wanted it to be. That is why it is possible for me to suspend all comprehension of our crowded, congested world and imagine the creek as the Delaware might have seen it ages ago – fertile and fishy. That is why, in the happy hours I spend there, I imagine it as the Last Best Place on Earth. I looked at the bank under the hemlocks, about three feet above the creek. There was a sunny spot, and I thought about wading to it, sitting down and lighting the cigar in my vest. But I kept fishing.

In the early 1990s, I started keeping a journal of Father's Day Creek, though I was pessimistic about ever finding a lot of trout there. After the state stopped stocking the creek, however, the meadow trail into the woods became overgrown with thorns and brush; each time I used it, I had to clear some of it. In all my trips to the stream since then, I have met only four other fishermen along its banks, and they used fly rods and returned any trout they caught.

One day, as I crossed the stream, I met a fellow with a British accent, and when I heard him speak I thought for a moment that the creek's reputation had somehow reached the land of chalk streams and Sir Izaak Walton, the 17th Century author of *The Compleat Angler*. I assumed I was in the company of an experienced angler.

The gentleman, who was dressed in waders and vest, seemed good-natured and mild-mannered. He asked if I had caught any trout. I reported having netted and released three small browns.

Predictably, the fellow wanted to know what fly I had been using to attract these trout, and I was more than happy to tell him.

"Adams parachute," I said, and that's shorthand for a common version of the most popular, versatile and effective dry fly in the angler's vest. "Adams Parachute" is not an entomological term. There is no aquatic insect called an Adams, much less one with a parachute. The fly is named after Charlie Adams, a Michigan man who in 1922 requested that his friend,

Leonard Halladay, design an all-purpose imitation of an adult mayfly. The parachute refers to a tuft of white animal hair, sometimes taken from a calf's tail, that makes it easier for the angler to see the fly as it drifts on the water.

"Oh," the British fellow said, "I didn't realize the Adams was hatching this time of year."

I just smiled at the realization that even polite British anglers are given to faking what they know, or never admitting what they don't. I gave him an Adams parachute from my fly box and wished him luck.

There are moments when you get to imagine the experience of the long-gone native Delaware. Like that time I waded into the waters of Father's Day Creek, above the gorge section, in the soft sunlight of a May afternoon, and ended up in locked stare with a whitetail deer, a buck that had had the same idea about walking into the creek moments before I did. There was no one else in sight, not a single sign of human activity – not a beer can, not a broken cinder block, not a shred of plastic. I heard nothing but river. No chainsaw in the woods. No jet in the sky. Not even the distant whine of highway traffic. It was just me and the river and the deer, and the deer drinking from the river.

He raised his head when he heard me, and water dripped off his chin. I froze in an awkward spot in the stream about 25 yards away. For about 30 seconds, he stared at me and I stared at him, a big-chested beast from the forest. I've seen plenty of deer in my travels, a common experience of Americans on the East Coast. By the late 20ᵗʰ Century, the whitetails seemed almost ubiquitous. I have seen them foraging near the Baltimore Beltway, on suburban streets and along country roads. When it seemed like a new and odd phenomenon, excited readers of *The Sun* would call me to report the news of hungry deer munching on shrubbery within the Baltimore city limits. I have spotted plenty in Pennsylvania, a lot of it road-kill. In fact, Pennsylvania and West Virginia lead the nation in motor vehicle encounters with deer. So telling you about a buck in Father's Day Creek is hardly the stuff of wilderness adventure. It's not as if I had encountered a grizzly.

But, in that setting of woods and water, absent any evidence of all the human activity that had occurred during the previous 400 years, it was possible to imagine being a hunter-gatherer from a nearby village of the Delaware. It was possible to imagine the once-upon-a-time world, before the Europeans arrived and started settling the land, cutting the trees, building cabins, tilling the soil and using the rivers for industry. It was possible, in that half-minute of a Tuesday in the 21ˢᵗ Century, to be just man and buck, locked in a primal stare, the hungry and the hunted. Before I could raise an imaginary bow and reach for an imaginary arrow in an imaginary quiver, the buck stepped to his right, deeper into the stream, where the water almost reached his withers, and he emerged dripping wet on the other side, shouldered through some bushes and disappeared into the sloping forest. There was no panic in his movement. His stride in the rushing water was powerful, purposeful and elegant. He seemed to me an old soul, a survivor, and I felt honored to have shared the water with him. I am pretty sure I whispered a thank-you, something like a prayer, for those 30 seconds on Father's Day Creek.

Beautiful and mysterious things sometimes happen like that – in flashes, out of nowhere, when you least expect them, leaving you stunned and awed.

One afternoon, while the sun was still fairly high, I came upon a village – a nursery, really – of Canada geese, those handsome birds with throats of black velvet. They had discovered the solitude and safety of Father's Day Creek long before I had. Their goslings ambled about the river bank, little tufts of brown fluff among the tall grass and fallen tree limbs. Off in a corner of the pool, about 30 yards away, was one white swan.

As if its mere floating presence wasn't impressive enough, the great bird decided I had come too close and, bobbing slightly forward, it began its ascent. With a ponderous grace, the bird spread its large wings, straightened its long neck and rose slowly off the water, away from the goose village, then climbed into the air above me. I stood still, silent and reverential. I could hear a soft whistle, like something from a quavering flute, as the mute swan's wings displaced air and powered away from me, high over the creek and the forested ridge beyond.

Another time, on another stream closer to home, I had an encounter with a stranger that turned into one of those remarkable moments in which something like the secret to happiness appears.

That sounds grandiose, but I think you know what I mean about moments like that. They're strange, beautiful epiphanies. Something happens – in the blink of an eye, in an act of kindness, in the sound of extraordinary music – that answers some question you've had about what it means not only to be human but to be happy about it.

It was 1996, and I was having one of my blue days – depressed or overworked or just bothered by something. I had to get away from the grind so I decided to go fishing in the Gunpowder River, about 20 miles north of Baltimore.

"Cheaper than going to a shrink," a fishing companion used to say.

I parked my car and hiked to a bridge over the river. I didn't feel like fishing right away. So I stood there, fly rod at rest, and watched the river flow. I turned when I heard a car approach. It was a silver Toyota Cressida. A large man in a polo shirt was at the wheel. I took him to be in his late 60s; he was handsome, in some aging-movie-star way, like Cesar Romero.

Our eyes met. He stopped the car and got out, a big barrel-chested man with wavy white hair and a sense of playfulness about him. He stepped toward me and pointed.

"You're Sicilian, aren't you?" he declared, in a big boom-box of a voice.

I didn't know what to say, except, "No," and that my mother's people were from the Naples area of Italy. My father was from Madeira, the Portuguese island off the coast of Morocco.

Good enough, the man said: Naples wasn't all that far from Sicily, and Sicily and Madeira were both islands.

Once the man was satisfied that we were somehow kindred, he shared personal information, and all in the next 60 seconds.

He told me that he was from Sicily, that he'd been a union truck driver, that he was an exceptional cook who made great spaghetti and meatballs, that he taught singing – cantors were among his students – and that he loved opera, and that he had quite a set of pipes, and would I like to hear him sing?

He didn't wait for the answer.

This big, jolly man gathered his breath, spread his arms, closed his eyes and, there on the bridge on a summer day, he started singing – to me, to the sky, to the trees, to the river, to the trout.

He sang in French, the baritone part from "Au Fond du Temple Saint," from Bizet's *The Pearl Fishers*.

Then he switched to Italian. I don't remember for certain what he sang. I might have challenged him to sing "Non Piu Andrai," which is the bass aria from the end of the first act of Mozart's *The Marriage of Figaro*.

But whatever it was that he sang, it was gorgeous – and delivered with theatrical panache.

Ladies and gents, this was no singing-in-the-shower voice. This was a professional voice, highly trained, with flashes of bravura. My God, we're standing on a bridge over the Gunpowder River, and here's this man with a rich, practiced baritone singing to a stranger out of pure and utter joy, as if his heart would burst otherwise.

It seemed to me that nothing in the world could ruin this man's day, and that he knew the answer to life's inevitable blues lurked in some deep place in the soul. Find that thing that makes you happy and call it up and never let go. Find that thing, and use it every day.

"If you don't use it, you'll lose it," he said of his singing voice.

This man turned out to be Casper Vecchione, something of a legend among serious singers and students in the Baltimore region, known for his big voice and big personality, a Renaissance man who drove a truck. I learned all this years later, after he died and members of his family contacted me. They had heard the story of Casper singing to a somber-looking newspaper columnist on the bridge over the Gunpowder River.

I learned that Casper had been a Sicilian immigrant, the son of a bootlegger, a student of the Peabody Conservatory of Music in Baltimore, veteran of World War II and a prisoner of war.

I can still hear Casper singing in Italian on the bridge. I thank him for singing the blues away on that summer day, and for teaching me, in a matter of minutes, something about how to be human and happy about it.

I tossed the Adams fly again and again, and, almost immediately, it attracted foot-long brown trout everywhere – in the shadows beneath overhanging rhododendron, in deep pockets behind boulders, in the white foam of riffles. I hooked small, frisky brook trout, too. They were all wild fish, not the hatchery-raised variety that awaited death further downstream at the hands of the bait anglers during the spring stocking season. I returned every fish I caught to the waters from which they came. I was excited and happy. The creek had never fished this well. That feeling of having discovered treasure stayed with me and, because it was Father's Day, I kept looking over my shoulder for another dad with a fishing rod. None ever appeared. I was alone in paradise. It was getting to be time for breakfast back at the house, and I was craving my father-in-law's galettes, the French version of pancakes. But I kept roaming and kept casting.

When my in-laws, Louie and Felicie, decided it was time to leave their retirement home in Pennsylvania, I felt sad, but also selfish, then guilty and foolish for feeling selfish. The departure from their paradise on the hill in Pennsylvania meant I no longer had an excuse, besides fishing in Father's Day Creek, to make the three-hour trip from Baltimore. It certainly would be harder to justify the drive. There were many other rivers to fish between here and there, requiring less travel and fewer carbon emissions. But my father-in-law's health had started to decline. Blessed with all-world, old-world common sense, he had made a tough decision –besides the one he made to leave France in 1950, the toughest in his life – to find a new, less isolated place that provided care as well as comfort. He was leaving paradise: a comfortable, yellow-brick rancher on seven acres surrounded by woods and meadows – "Like old country" – for a modern house in a smartly-planned retirement community closer to Baltimore.

And so, in the early summer of 2004, when I otherwise would have been fishing in the creek, I found myself immersed in a ritual. I had heard other baby boomers speak of this time, and now it was mine – time to help the Greatest Generation move to the next horizon.

It was a gloomy day, about a week before the movers were to come, and I stood in Louie's workshop, which was lined floor to ceiling with steel and wooden tools, some of them handmade, from his 50 years as the family's chief handyman. I held a heavy, gritty, oily object in my hands – a belt grinder – and my father-in-law, who could no longer lift the thing himself, announced that it must go to the new house in the retirement community.

"They don't make them like that anymore," he said. "You don't want to throw a thing like that away. You know how much something like that cost today? Put 'em in the box."

I placed the motor and the grinder in a wooden wine crate. My hands were dirty. I wiped them on a rag, also dirty. Louie directed me to the next object, also a grinder.

"This one is even better than the other one," he said. "I sharpen all my knives with that. Put 'em in the box."

"You know what *that* is?" Louie asked, pointing to a foot-wide wooden spool of white wire, enough for a full run through an apartment complex.

"Telephone wire?" I guessed.

"That's it. Put 'em in the box."

Everything that was to go to the new place went in boxes.

Everything staying behind – to be sold to neighbors, or left by the roadside for scavengers – went on a trailer outside the workshop. The trailer filled slowly. Louie could not seem to part with much.

"Are you sure you want all this?" I asked, pointing to a patch of neatly wrapped nylon ropes hanging in a corner of the shop. "And what about all these extension cords?"

"Put 'em in the box."

Though I had an itch to, I did not try to talk him out of taking all those items to the new place. I could tell Louie was in deep sorrow about the move – "Is not my house anymore," he said at one point – so I was careful to be quiet and obedient. I did not ask questions, unless I had something to say that might cheer him up.

"Louie," I said, "you remember the blue pliers?"

He laughed. It was a summer day probably 20 years earlier, and Louie, on his knees by his tractor, needed to remove a cotter pin from the mower deck of his Wheel Horse lawn tractor. He told me, in his still-thick French accent, to fetch "blue pliers" from the workshop. Eager to please, I did as told. But I could not find blue pliers. There was good reason: The pliers had not been blue in years, the enamel having worn off the handles long before I assumed the role of earnest son-in-law. For years it remained a little joke – a simple, old-country farmer joke – between us.

To call Louie a handyman was really to demean him. He was a chef in New York City, having worked up from immigrant pantry help in the hotels of Manhattan to the Harvard Club and the executive dining room at Morgan Stanley. There, he could order anything for his menus because, as he said through his thick accent, "At Morgan Stanley, money is no objection." The daily clientele included international financiers, bankers and sometimes heads of state. One day in the 1980s, Louie prepared lunch for Richard M. Nixon. After dessert, the former president autographed Louie's toque blanche.

At his weekend place in Pennsylvania, Louie showed me how to work a chain saw and chop word, prune fruit trees and grow potatoes, dry and preserve onions, slice a turkey and poach a salmon, replace a fan belt, make a Manhattan, play bocce, win at Uno, fold linen napkins for formal dining, prepare a family picnic, install an electrical outlet, insulate and panel a club basement, grow endive in the dark, can vinegar peppers, build shelves for a wine cellar and how to tie bulky objects to a car roof. He could make a laundry basket out of forsythia branches. He could install plumbing and electrical systems, and did so in two houses – the tenement he had bought and renovated in Queens 50 years earlier, and his weekend/retirement house in Pennsylvania.

Louie had joie de vivre to the nth power, an extravagantly generous spirit and a personality much bigger than his body. Everyone around him seemed to gain energy from him.

He was a farm boy from France, though he was always quick to specify Brittany as his place of birth. He and his wife, Felicie, grew up speaking Breton, a Celtic language. They survived Nazi occupation and war, then moved to the United States in the 1950s, arriving in New York, Louie liked to remind us, "with a wooden suitcase, a new wife and $100." He also brought a vigorous attitude, an awesome determination to succeed and the countless skills he had learned on his parents' farm.

He went to work in hotel kitchens, putting in long hours to learn and refine his craft and save money for the house in Queens. He was proud of that.

Louie admired John F. Kennedy, but he had voted for Nixon in 1968 and 1972, and he was a big fan of Ronald Reagan. That led to some challenging conversations, especially after a couple of Manhattans.

Louie believed in saving money and never buying something unless you had the cash for it.

He also believed:

* The best way to avoid speeding tickets – and just getting off with a warning – was to cover your Buick with the stickers of every police union and chiefs of police association between New York and Florida.

* Keeping knives sharp at all times reduced frustration in kitchens by 80 percent.

* Taking time to sit and eat a home-cooked meal, every day, no matter how busy you are, makes you healthier.

He was a thoroughly charming man who, upon being introduced to a stranger, could make that person feel like the most important one in the room. I knew Louie long enough to also see his temperamental side, so I was glad to just be his son-in-law and not his sous chef. But, as passionate as he was about getting the consomme correct or the firewood stacked smartly, he maintained a joyous nature, and we could all learn something from that: Be passionate about what you do, and don't forget joy.

On weekends in Pennsylvania, Louie was a top-flight organic gardener. He rendered fabulous meals from the vegetables in his garden and from a wild animal that he or Pierre might have shot. The centerpiece of one Thanksgiving dinner was a wild turkey that had made the mistake of roosting in a tree by Louie's driveway.

Now, as he packed to leave for good, the large garden was done. All it offered was asparagus and volunteer lettuce. Louie had not had the strength for the garden since the chemotherapy started. "If I knew it would make me feel like an old man, I never would have done it," he said when we broke for lunch.

Afterwards, while Louie took a nap, I sat on a bench in a storage shed and, looking down, noticed a fat stack of manila papers, something like baccalaureate programs, bundled smartly with butcher twine, the way Louie, the chef, might have tied up a roast. They were the luncheon menus from his last job, when he cooked for millionaires and billionaires at Morgan Stanley. He had saved them all and had taken them home when he retired. The bundle was tied so firmly I could read only the top card, for Tuesday June 4, 1985. That day, Louie had prepared duck pate, chilled potage Senegalaise, cold medallions of veal Florentine, broiled sea scallops, lamb chops, poached halibut filet, a salad of escarole and mushrooms, a dessert of fresh melon, berries and ice cream.

There were hundreds of menus in the stack. It felt dense and heavy in my hands. I realized that what I held was a big part of a man's life, the day-after-day of proud work. Everything I touched in Louie's private spaces – the ropes and motors and wrenches, rolls of burlap and hatchets and pliers – all of them felt that way, heavy with time, saturated with a man's ambitions and dreams.

I had truly been blessed to have such a great man for a father-in-law. Our relationships with two of the primary men in our lives – fathers and fathers-in-law – can get complicated, and I have heard them described in multiple ways:

- "My father was, or is, the greatest guy who ever lived, followed immediately by my father-in-law, the second-greatest guy who ever lived."

- "My relationship with my father was terrible, but I married well and got the greatest father-in-law a fellow could imagine."

- "My father and I have always had a great relationship, but my father-in-law is a pain, and the less time I spend with him the better."

- "I get along with neither my father nor father-in-law very well. I'm a two-time loser when it comes to father figures."

Of course, there's another option: "None of the above." Several years ago, during a breakfast with some friends as Father's Day approached, I got responses that did not fit any of the four choices I just listed.

"I barely knew my old man," said one. "I did not know my father-in-law very well, either. I grew up without a father image. My notion of fatherhood is a composite of men I knew, and not necessarily well."

Another said: "My father ran out on us when I was a kid, and my wife's father did the same to her family. From what I've heard, both of us are lucky, and we have created a whole happy life together without those losers."

But for those who had both father and father-in-law, it can be a mixed bag of blessings and challenges. It's tricky social science – trying to measure, categorize or describe the relationships between fathers and sons in comparison with fathers-in-law and sons-in-law. In my experience, this is one of the most fraught subjects of all among men, something I could not even acknowledge, never mind discuss, while my father was alive, or even for several years after his death in 1986.

In one major respect, the comparison is wholly unfair because the relationships are wholly unequal. Most of us have known, or knew, our fathers since we were toddlers and did not know our fathers-in-law until we were adults; one relationship is loaded with emotional baggage while the other is comparatively new and psychologically clean.

As Louie and I prepared things for his move to the retirement community – his tools, hardware, furniture, photographs, bocce balls – we tripped through a lot of back-story about the family's time at their Pennsylvania retreat. It made me sad. It made me worry – that selfish feeling – that I would not get to Father's Day Creek as much. But, more than anything, those reflections left me keenly grateful for the special relationship I had had with this man.

Not that I needed a melancholy experience like packing to appreciate him.

I had felt blessed from the beginning. Louie was funny, jolly, considerate, talented, generous, wise and strong. According to Geoffrey Greif, an associate dean of the University of Maryland School of Social Work and author of books on fatherhood, it was no accident I came into this. "It's not random," Greif told me. "Men are sometimes attracted to a woman because of the woman's father, especially if there's a father void in the man's life, and he's looking to fill it."

If I had to answer my own Pops Quiz, I'd take answer No. 2, difficult as it is to admit. I mean no disrespect to my father, Joe, who had a tough life long before he became a parent, and long after, and who lived too much of it angrily, and who died before we could finish fixing the broken bridges between us. But I had a much more pleasing and rewarding relationship with my father-in-law. There's no getting around that. My father was acutely aware of – and, I believe, jealous of – my good relationship with Louie, to the point where I could not comfortably talk about my wife's father in Joe's presence. I was always careful not to compare the men. My kids came to appreciate Joe, the grandfather they never knew, as a hard-working immigrant who suffered a lot of setbacks: The death of his father when Joe was 14, being forced to leave school and work to support his widowed mother, subjected to various humiliations as he grew up poor and fatherless, suffering serious spinal injuries related to his work, and years later losing his business in a fire. I never compared Joe to Louie, the man my kids knew only as a funny and playful grandfather who stuck 10-dollar bills in their pockets.

My father-in-law was not perfect, but he came as close to the ideal father as any man I knew, and I would tell him that on Father's Day. Of course, had I grown up in Louie's house – and not joined his life in progress when I was already a young adult and he was a middle-aged man – things might have been different. But I doubt it. I don't worry about that might-have-been anyway. I take gratefully what was handed to me, and I consider it a blessing. I think of Louie, and of these things, every time I fish on Father's Day Creek.

While I loved my father despite our problems and learned some life lessons from him, I would have been a different man and parent had it not been for the example of my father-in-law. A father makes a difference. So can a father-in-law, and mine did.

The results of Father's Day 2000 were impressive, but not shocking. There had been a slow buildup to it. I had kept notes about the creek in a journal. Each year after the stocking stopped there were more brown trout in the feeding lanes of the river, and each year the fish I caught were longer and fatter. In this delicate and beautiful place, progress was measured in inches. On Father's Day 1993, I caught only six-inch brown trout, what my father would call "dinky fish." In 1997, I caught 12-inch browns and, in 1999, I caught one at 14 inches. In 1994, I hooked only two trout on Father's Day, but in 1998 I caught 10. I caught native brook trout, too, and small, stream-bred rainbows. This progress was not about me and my still-developing skills as a fly angler, it was about Father's Day Creek and its resiliency. Here was mounting proof: Left alone, unmolested by invading hatchery trout and indiscriminate fish killers, the stream-born trout grew and thrived. This eco-renaissance made me feel even more protective of the creek. I made a point of never telling Pierre or his friend, Roger, about the river's comeback, lest they plunder with brass and bait what had become a great river for fly-fishing. Same with my father-in-law, though he was never as gung-ho about killing little fish as Pierre was. The sun was moving above treetops now, so I started hiking downstream, back toward the bridge and my car, casting in spots that looked good, but for the moment raising no additional trout.

As much as I enjoyed fishing alone on Father's Day Creek – having the whole place to myself – the experience took on bigger meaning when my son, Nick, could fish it with me, and with a fly rod.

A word or two about that:

Dads want their sons and daughters to experience some of same good things they experienced growing up, and fishing is one of them. It's not for everyone, but you never know what a kid is going to like until they try it. Some things stick, a lot of things don't. Without being pushed, Nick became an excellent fly angler and, by the time he was 18, he was out-fishing me.

However, had you judged by his first fishing experience, you never would have predicted that.

When he was three years old, he hooked a large, fat brook trout in Mike Flanagan's spring-fed pond, and after we landed it, I held it close to Nick so Mike could get a photograph. Mike leaned in with the camera. Nick shrieked. His eyes filled with terror. He ran for his mother. He wanted nothing to do with the monster in my hands. "Scarred for life," Mike said, in his droll New England way. I worried he might have been correct.

Nick's younger sister, Julia, on the other hand, along with Mike's daughter, Kendall, enjoyed catching fish and holding them in their little hands before releasing them. They smiled through the whole thing and gladly posed for pictures. But, as much as Julia seemed to enjoy catching fish when she was four or five, she showed little interest in it as a young adult. She prefered to just come along on fishing trips as official photographer.

The key to this, first of all, is getting kids interested in the outdoors. Surveys in recent years show a big disconnect between children and nature. The Outdoors Foundation poll of 2014 found that an astonishing 40 percent of kids between 13 and 17 had no experiences in the outdoors within the previous year. And outdoors participation falls steadily as Americans age; only 37 percent of people over 45 reported an outdoor activity in the foundation poll. This is not a good thing. The less time people spend in natural settings – woods, trails, rivers, mountains, bays – the less they care about them, heightening the risk that those places will be abused and exploited. And you don't get to have a "spirit-home" in the hereafter unless you establish one in the here and now.

My interest in the outdoors and nature did not come from a parent – unless you credit my mother for kicking us out of the house each day in summer. She did not take us camping; she did not own a canoe. She just expected us to stay outdoors and stay busy, coming home only for lunch and supper. So we rode our bikes, went fishing, played baseball, built forts in the woods, made it all up as we went along.

By the time I was an adult working in the news business, I had become too busy for nature hikes or other adventures; my fishing time was limited to a few outings each year. But having kids changed that. And so I can say this: Taking your son or daughter, nephew or niece – or borrowing a friend's or neighbor's kid – for a visit to a state park gives you an opportunity to discover or rediscover your inner outdoorsman.

Before I took Nick fishing, we kept it simple and went for hikes. I made notes of what happened when we walked a fire trail in the watershed near one of the reservoirs that supply water to Baltimore. Nick was five at the time. It was the autumn of 1995. We saw common birds – six blue jays squawking in a row of birches, nuthatches scampering down tree trunks, woodpeckers, titmice, juncos, chickadees, sparrows, finches, starlings and grackles. And three bluebirds. The latter were amazing, like the king's colorful coachmen hustling through a feudal forest. The royal blue on the male's back can take your breath away, especially when it appears suddenly among the bare bones of trees or against a slope of fallen leaves. I told Nicholas that, when I was his age, I never saw bluebirds. But they had made a comeback in the East and become more abundant. When I see one now, it makes me happy, even hopeful. "When I see a bluebird," Nick said, "it makes me want to eat a blueberry muffin."

We saw a chipmunk scamper along a little brook. We saw turkey vultures picking at the carcass of a deer. The birds were large and comical, hopping about, stretching their featherless necks, picking at the dried meat on the deer's rib cage. We saw a great blue heron descend through an opening in the trees, land along a creek and start his vigil for food that swims. We saw a trout rise to feed on a tiny black fly known as a midge. We heard the crash of a startled deer in the woods, its hoofs cracking small branches and rustling leaves. We never saw the deer. Nicholas squeezed my hand.

We heard the honking of Canada geese and looked up at a pink, late-summer sky and saw two chevrons arching to the west. We heard, but never found, a woodpecker at work on some high mast in the woods.

All of that made Nicholas comfortable and interested in spending more time outdoors, and it was fishing that usually took us there.

As eager as I was to see him try the fly rod, he did not seem physically capable of the cast until he was about 10 years old. So I bought him a lightweight spinning rod until he was ready to fish on the fly.

If you want to get your children started in fishing, remember: It's important that they catch something, and you should release what they catch. Take them to a pond with bluegill, or one stocked with trout, and try to use lures with barbless hooks. (Use needle-nose pliers to tamp the barbs down.) Skip the worms. Bluegills and stocked trout often suck worms deep inside and it's almost impossible to remove the hook without causing a fatality. Artificial baits with barbless hooks save lives. Your kids can release the fish they catch back to the water without guilt.

Another thing to remember: You do not get to fish. When they are little, kids require too much attention, and if you want them to have fun and actually catch something, you have to serve as their guide and teacher. When they run off to check out the polliwogs and hunt for turtles, you might get a few minutes to make a few casts. Otherwise, you should consider the fishing day theirs, not yours. The day will come when you and your son or daughter can fish together, without your constant attention.

For Nick and me, that day came when he was 12 years old, and he had become competent as a caster of flies. We drove a long and meandering country road to the North Branch of the Potomac River in Barnum, West Virginia. Just as we arrived, at about 8 am on a Monday in June 2002, I noticed several trout rising in a long pool to a hatch of mayflies. Perfect. I tied the all-purpose Adams fly to Nick's line and, for the first time, told him to wade into the river ahead of me and cast to the rises. Until that point, I had almost always stood to his side or behind him when he fished in moving water. On this day, he took my instruction and, without hesitation, waded to a point where the water was at his waist. He managed to keep his arms high and make good casts upstream. On the second cast, he hooked an exquisite brown trout, 14 inches long and chunky. It was Nick's first trout on a dry fly. He played the fish well, following my advice about keeping his hands high and avoiding slack in the line. We netted the brown, admired him and released him. I might have been more excited than Nick was. I had taught my son to fish with a fly rod and he had had the optimum experience – a trout taking a dry off the surface – at the age of 12. I assumed he would be smitten with the sport for life and, as of this writing, 16 years later, he still enjoys fly fishing, and even gets a little frustrated when he gets skunked. We go to Father's Day Creek together at least once a year, and while prospecting for brookies, browns and rainbows in a small Pennsylvania stream does not approach, in spectacle or expense, the big fishing adventures associated with Montana or Alaska, it serves us as father and son just fine. I feel like a wealthy man when my son fishes with me.

I also feel like a wealthy man when, in my quiet time alone on Father's Day Creek, I count up the good friends and mentors I had over the years. This is an accounting that's worth doing now and then, and it's often on Father's Day, reflecting on the absence of my father and the older men who once surrounded me and encouraged me, that I count up my life's fortune.

"He will not miss the hunter's satisfaction; every moment of his pursuit will reward his pains with some delight, and he will have reason to think his time not ill-spent, even when he cannot much boast of a great acquisition."

– John Locke, British philosopher

Sometimes the fly angler gets hooked into a fishing trip low in nature – in my case, anything that involves bait or chum, big engines and trolling – but you go to be sociable. A friend invites you, so you go. Fly fishing is not for everyone, and you don't want to be a snob and confirm the classic suspicions about people who fish that way.

One time, my friend Tom "Bush Hog" James organized a week-long trip to a beach house in Hatteras, North Carolina, advertising it to me and two other colleagues from the *Baltimore Evening Sun* newsroom as "surf fishing the Outer Banks." But surf fishing in the Bush Hog style was all about luck and location. You had to rent a beach house where you think the fish would be during your vacation because the strategy – if that's the word for it – calls for walking 200 paces from the house, deploying your beach chair, sticking your rod holder in the sand, and hoping that a blitz of bluefish or striped bass will take place within 100 yards of where you have planted your ass. That was Bush Hog's plan – sit, wait, drink cheap and often – and he wanted us to know, on the first day of fishing, that, as he was in command and this was his strategy, we should keep our expectations low.

"Sit down, take it easy," he said. "Fishin' ain't catchin'."

That meant we were going to spend quality time together; we would talk about guy stuff. After an eight-hour road trip to Hatteras, we were not about to pile back into Michael Wheatley's rusted Chevy Blazer and drive the shoreline looking for blitzing blues, which is what successful surf fishing entails. Wheatley, Bush Hog, Nick Yengich and I were going to sit right in front of the beach house and wait for the fish to come to us. We would cast monstrous hooks heavily baited with razor clams and weighted with lead into the surf, with distance in casting prized above finesse, and we would leave the lines offshore indefinitely. Hooking a fish could take a day, or several days, or it might never happen. It did not matter. We were not going on the hunt for fish, not going to drive the beach like the bloodthirsty locals with their SUVs, pickup trucks and campers bristling with 11-foot surf rods and outfitted with CB radios and coolers on tailgate racks.

"Fishin' ain't catchin'," Bush Hog said again, and we settled down in the sand like plovers at his feet. I kept an eye on my rod for signs of a strike, but I dialed back my ambitions for the week.

Not that there's anything wrong with that.

To enjoy fishing with friends, you have to reduce your expectations a bit and put more effort into the social aspect of the sport. Some guys approach fishing as if it were a weekend job, or a project at work; it all gets very scientific and precise and they do not seem to take much pleasure in it. If they do not complete the mission – no fish for their investment of time and material – they get cranky and frustrated. In Bush Hog's presence, and under his guidance, I was disabused of the idea that catching fish was necessary for a good experience in the surf, or really anywhere.

Another time he suggested that we go fishing in one of the public reservoirs near Baltimore. It's hard to do that without a boat, but I agreed to go. I knew what I was getting into. I had to leave the fly rod home, and take a spinning rod and a folding chair. With Bush Hog, being there was what mattered – not the harvest.

Fishing with the Hog meant bait and wait. He used everything from worms to Green Giant Brand Whole Kernel Niblets Sweet Corn. He once used a leftover pierogi from St. Michael's Ukrainian Catholic Church in East Baltimore, rolling pieces of it into bait balls and casting it into a pond. We caught crappie with it.

Preparing for a trip to Liberty Reservoir, I went to a tackle shop. While I was there, a fellow came in and inquired as to the best catfish bait on the market. The big guy behind the counter, who was bagging night crawlers, nodded in the general direction of an aisle in the store and said: "Earthworm hot dogs. They're really hittin' 'em." Somebody – I'm guessing a bait chemist in New Jersey – had come up with the idea of taking essence of earthworm, along with some actual earthworm meat and other ingredients, running all of it through a sausage extruder, forming it into the shape of hot dogs, slicing them up and packing them in jars. The labels on the jars said, "Not for human consumption." And good thing because Bush Hog might have been tempted.

He was like that. He enjoyed all sorts of culinary exotica on our fishing adventures on rocking charter boats on the Chesapeake Bay: Raw oysters, orange beef-lip sausage in brine, hot salsa and Velveeta balls, pickled onions and eggs.

Our Sunday morning outing to the reservoir began with a stop at a convenience store, where Bush Hog purchased some of that dark brown, wrinkled beef jerky that comes in vacuum-wrapped plastic with an expiration date beyond human life expectancy. These morsels were the size and shape of strips of bacon, about 7 inches long, and they fit perfectly in a horizontal, zippered pocket in Bush Hog's L.L. Bean fishing vest.

"If it fits, eat it," Bush Hog said.

We went down to the reservoir, through the woods and onto some rocks at water's edge. There were a few men and boys on the opposite shore. It was quiet, warm and sunny. Canada geese flew by, the sunlight shimmering on their backs, their wingtips snapping at the surface of the water.

Bush Hog and I, as always, were more interested in talking politics than fishing, more interested in catching up than catching fish. But on that particular Sunday morning, ours was not the only bonding going on. We heard one, then two, then three and four and five big splashes along the shore. I thought someone was throwing rocks into the reservoir. But it was carp. Hundreds of them. They were in pairs, parked in water a couple of inches deep, flipping and flapping and splashing in a raw and primal mating festival. The male carp were eager to get things going so they pushed the females with their noses and fins to encourage spawning, and the females jumped and splashed to release and spread their eggs. We were astonished by the scope of the spectacle. "Amazing," Bush Hog said. "Who knew carp were into dirty dancing?"

Next thing I noticed was a big stick floating about 60 feet off the shore. There was a black lump on the stick. And the lump had a neck. And the neck had a head. A turtle had crawled up on the stick. There was a mild current and light breeze in the middle of the reservoir, and in a matter of minutes the current had moved the big stick with the turtle 100 yards to our right. The turtle was riding the wave. Bush Hog was impressed. "Amazing," he said. "Who knew turtles were into surfing?" He unzipped the pocket in his fishing vest, pulled out the beef jerky, tore at the plastic wrapper with his teeth and bit into that finely cured meat. We spent the rest of the morning watching the turtle surfing in the middle of the reservoir, listening to the carp dirty dancing along the shore, chewing the fat and chewing beef jerky. We did not catch fish. Catching fish was never the point.

– 8:50 am

I reached the spot on Father's Day Creek known as the swimming hole. It's a deep pool downstream of the gorge, near a clearing where, over the years, some of the locals had picnics and campfires. Someone had built a bench between two trees and, once upon a time, there was a rope swing that carried boys and girls over the pool. The pool at the swimming hole is a fly fishing challenge. More like a nightmare. The currents are quirky and difficult to master. Instead of floating in a straight line, your fly will drift this way and that before curling back upstream. On Father's Day 2000, I walked right past the place. Some places just aren't worth the frustration, especially if you're still learning how to cast effectively. Besides, the fishing had been too good over the previous hour. Why spoil the morning with frustrating casts into the screwy swimming hole? There was a nice pool downstream that I wanted to reach before breakfast back at the house, so I headed there.

Among my most important fishing companions were Bill Burton and Calvert Bregel, best friends and fellow travelers on land and sea, older men who treated me as they might have a favorite nephew.

Bill was the bearded, pipe-smoking outdoors editor of *The Evening Sun* in Baltimore for 37 years; he fished with presidents and professional athletes. He was a prolific writer and broadcaster, a well-traveled chronicler of sportfishing and hunting, a real hustler. He took me on trips throughout the Chesapeake Bay, in the Atlantic, and in the bass ponds of southern Maryland. He gave me the little book of Native American wisdom that I keep in my fishing vest to this day.

Calvert was a Baltimore attorney who, with his father and partner, had a reputation for getting excellent settlements in divorces. Their clients included the wives of some of Maryland's wealthiest men and a few celebrities, including Mickey Rooney, Hedda Hopper, Dorothy Lamour and Johnny Unitas. Calvert was a true bon vivant; he loved hunting, fishing, chasing and charming women. He was a country squire, tennis player, sailor, practical joker, card shark, conspiracy theorist, founding member of the Playboy Club in Baltimore and mixer of outstanding Bloody Marys. His fishing boat was called the Miss Demeanor.

Bill and Calvert were about the same age. Calvert joined the merchant marine after prep school, near the end of World War II. Bill ran away from home and joined the Seabees in the Pacific toward the war's end.

Calvert had handled Bill's legal affairs. They became fast and full friends, and they stayed that way for decades. I envied and enjoyed their friendship – the stories, the playful sarcasm and jokes, the laughter, the interest they took in each other's families, their almost daily contact, their trips together. They invited me along on some of their adventures, including a journey to Arlington, Vermont, where Bill had spent his high school years.

A Rhode Island native, Bill left home when his father refused to let him join the Navy during the war. On his way to Canada to sign up with the Royal Canadian Air Force, Bill stopped in Vermont to visit his aunt and uncle, MiMi and Larry Brush. They talked their nephew into staying with them to finish high school before enlisting.

Fifty years later, Calvert and I visited Arlington with Bill. The idea was to do some trout fishing in the famous Battenkill, the river that ran through the town. We were to sleep and take our meals at the home of Bill's elderly relatives. When Aunt MiMi and Uncle Larry came out to greet us in the driveway of their white colonial, they were nice as can be, and they struck me as runners-up for selection as the ma-and-pa figures in Grant Wood's "American Gothic." Turns out, the Brushes had appeared in a famous painting: Norman Rockwell's "The Country Doctor," which became a *Saturday Evening Post* cover in 1947. Rockwell had a studio in Arlington, and the Brushes knew him. They had posed with their infant daughter for "The Country Doctor."

Aunt MiMi and Uncle Larry were pleasant and practical New Englanders who kept a firm daily schedule.

Saturday breakfast, for instance, was to be 8:30 a.m. Sharp.

"Oh, no, Burton, do we have to have breakfast?" Calvert moaned as we drove to the river at 7 a.m.

"Yes, Bregel," Burton said. "Aunt MiMi wants to make us a big breakfast."

"But I want to do some fishing," Calvert replied, betraying slight annoyance at having to start fishing, then stop to sit in a house with too many doilies and eat what would certainly be a too-long breakfast. It was the typical kind of good-natured, old-friends grousing that went on between Calvert and Bill on fishing trips.

"I don't want to seem ungracious, but my goodness, Burton, we came here to do some fishing and we haven't caught anything yet."

"I have," I said from the back seat of Calvert's Ford Explorer, as he pulled into a parking space by a bridge over the Battenkill.

"Yeah, when we weren't looking, you did," Calvert said. "Burton, do we have to have breakfast?"

"Indulge me, Bregel. Just go along with it, will you?"

It was an exquisite morning, the early sunlight on the foliage, and the slightest chill in the air. Calvert pulled on his waders, and set up his fly rod and tied on a fly I had suggested: a beadhead prince nymph. This process – the donning of waders and boots, the assembling of the rod, the threading of its eyes with the fly line, the attaching to that fly line the proper monofilament leader and to that leader the correct tippet and to that tippet the nymph imitation – took close to 25 minutes.

It was 7:30 before Calvert actually stepped into the Battenkill.

Another five minutes later, on his second or third cast, he lost his nymph in an overhead tree.

Another five minutes passed before I could get to him and tie another fly to his tippet.

In the next 30 minutes nothing of consequence occurred. No fish were hooked.

"Beautiful morning," Calvert said, always appreciative of the natural world around him.

Just then a young woman appeared, as if from nowhere. She was in her 20s, extremely attractive, with dark brown hair tied in a ponytail. She wore waders and a fishing vest, and she clutched a clipboard.

"Well now, Dan," Calvert said. "Will you look at that?"

"I'm looking, Calvert."

The young woman drew closer. Calvert's playboy eyes went on red alert.

"How are you gentlemen doing?" the young woman called from the high stream bank.

"You must have us mistaken for someone else," Calvert said, and the young woman laughed.

"I'm doing a creel survey for the state of Vermont Department of Fisheries Management," she said, "And I'd like to ask you a few questions. May I approach?"

"Please do," Calvert said, winking at me, reaching for her and helping the young woman down the stream bank into the water. "You stand right here and ask me your questions, my dear."

It was obvious by now that Calvert Bregel, outdoorsman and ladies' man, was in the hunt. What I heard from a distance of about 20 feet was Calvert asking the young woman twice as many questions as she asked him, and from the corner of my eye it became increasingly clear that Calvert was quite taken with her and she quite charmed by Calvert.

I continued fishing without success, watching and listening to a master at work in the next pool, admiring his craft, his way with words and with women, in this case one in her mid-20s. Calvert never acted his age, and often it was to his benefit.

He had just arrived at important questions – "Do you live far from here?" "What time do you finish work?" – when Bill Burton could be heard calling, first from a distance, then through the bushes directly behind and above us, on the high stream bank.

"Bregel! Time for breakfast!"

Burton's plea stopped Calvert in mid-sentence.

"Come on, Bregel, Aunt MiMi's waiting."

Calvert was crestfallen. It was time to leave the river, remove the bulky waders and head back to the house for the big New England breakfast. But Calvert had not completed his mission. He had not caught a fish nor had he sufficient time to work his magic on the young woman. She hadn't given him her phone number.

Burton's words from the bushes, "Aunt MiMi's waiting" seemed to be the young woman's cue to evacuate.

We returned back to the house near the center of Arlington. Calvert, a bit sullen, sat across from me at an elegantly set dining room table. Breakfast was large and delicious. But poor Calvert. I had never seen a fellow more wistful as he sat through a meal, slowly chewing Aunt Mimi's French toast, and day-dreaming about the one that got away.

I fished Father's Day Creek at the invitation of a landowner, portly and affable Sammy. Sammy is a jack-of-all trades who made his living from contracts for the small-scale manufacturing of machine parts. He bought several acres of woods, cleared some of it, built a house and large workshop, and created a playland for his children – a barn and paddock for his horse-loving daughter, a dirt-bike course for his son. The dirt-bike course was a trail on a grassy hill leading to the creek; the trail wound through a small meadow and a stretch of woods, then up another hill to the high ridge along the gorge. The trail included a couple of berms for jumps.

For a few years, it seemed Sammy's son, Mark, used the trail every time I used the river, and, of course, the sound of a dirt bike, a few decibels higher than a chainsaw, disturbed the peace. Still, you don't complain to the management when the fishing is free. I even came to appreciate what Sammy and Mark had: a relationship built on mutual respect for the internal combustion engine.

Sammy was a motor head – he had cars, pickup trucks, a motorboat and a Harley-Davidson – and his teenaged son had come to love the same toys. They spent hours together working on them, and Sammy liked to tell stories of high-speed thrills. This looked like textbook father-son bonding through teaching and shared experience: The father shows the boy the way – how to change the oil in a car, how to bait a hook – and the boy attempts to emulate and please the father. All boys will go along with this for a while; they have little choice. Some turn from the father's way sooner than others, seeking independence. But some pick up the hobby – motors, firearms, fishing, football, grilling meats – and never let go.

I envied Sammy and his son their bond, one I never had with my father. Our best times together had been on the *Nan-Sue*, but those times were too rare.

So, decades later, when I fished Father's Day Creek and heard the growl of a dirt bike, I quietly envied

Sammy's son. It seemed he had been given the great gift of a clever, good-natured father who enjoyed, perhaps above all else, showing his son how to change the air filter in a truck or clean the fuel line in an outboard motor. Sammy was father, mentor and teacher – never aloof, always present, showing the way. And he had created a place for his son to have adventures on wheels well before he was old enough to drive on the public roads.

Of course, I don't know the full story. I was an interloper, a neighbor's son-in-law who showed up a few times each year to fish. But at least that is how the relationship appeared to me. And it is why, for a while, I thought about avoiding, rather than embracing, Father's Day Creek on Father's Day.

A phone call on a spring day told of Mark's sudden and shocking death. He had been on a motorcycle, less than two miles from his house, and had slammed into a car at an intersection. Death was immediate. It happened on a Sunday evening in May, four days short of Mark's 19th birthday. I never inquired about the details of the accident and knew little beyond what I read in the local paper. I never spoke to Sammy or his wife at any length about the searing, life-sucking pain it caused them. It was too much to even contemplate: Every parent's nightmare, the horrible breaking of the father-son bond I had seen from a short distance, the fact that it happened on wheels, and to a young man with a promising future. "A man is not supposed to bury his son," wailed the father of a college chum who had died at 21 of Hodgkin's disease. That's a cry you never forget. A bitter, despondent cry.

Over the years, I have interviewed numerous men and women who had lived through the death of a child – some from the awful street violence afflicting Baltimore; some lost in rowhouse fires; three who had died in the 9/11 terrorist attacks; one slain in prison; several killed fighting the country's wars, from Vietnam to Iraq. Those stories became harder to write after I had children of my own. In fact, for a time after I became a father, I tried to avoid tales of boys and girls dying young.

But there was no avoiding the sudden death of Sammy's son, and the end to all I had witnessed on my visits to their family compound in the Pennsylvania mountains. As the years went by, weeds and small trees grew on the dirt bike trail, and the berm was reduced to a grassy bump on my hike to the creek. I think of the boy every time I travel to Sammy's place. For years, I passed a stop sign adorned with ribbons, plastic flowers and a Mylar balloon to mark the spot where Mark had died. Every time I hike down to the creek through Sammy's woods, I step, with a kind of haunted reverence, around the berm. I count a lot of blessings when I approach the creek and wade into its cool waters, and among them the blessing of life and of fatherhood.

One Sunday morning in June, 10 years after Mark's death, my son Nick joined me for the annual trip to Father's Day Creek. When we arrived, Sammy, by then divorced and living alone, came out to greet us. He had not been expecting to see my son, who by then was 26. Sammy was not the old Sammy. He was diminished – still affable, but in what seemed like a forced way, designed to cover pain. He frowned and squinted into the sun and told us to have a good time in the creek. The memory of Mark came up with the soft breeze. It was right there with us. It was Father's Day, of course, and my son and I thanked Sammy for access to the river from his property, then headed silently down the old bike trail to fish in the creek.

One of the great things about fly fishing is the hiking. You don't sit on a cooler waiting for a nibble on your line. You are on your feet the whole time, casting to different fishy-looking spots from different angles. The course of the creek is varied – from the long stretch at the bottom of the rhododendrum slope to the gorge with its deceivingly high cliff face to the long, open run through the hemlock grove. On Father's Day 2000, headed downstream, on my way back to the car, I walked through the woods, careful to keep my fly rod from snapping against a tree. I heard a blue jay squawk, a chickadee chirp, and a couple of crows cackle. I saw a chipmunk scurry out of my path. I smelled honeysuckle and felt a cooling breeze. I soon reached the one last spot I wanted to fish before heading back to the house for Father's Day breakfast. The spot looked as alluring as ever, and even a little spooky.

In 2007, I decided to ask readers of my *Baltimore Sun* column to send me lists of "things I learned from my father" so I might publish a selection of them on Father's Day. In soliciting comments, I said anything goes, good or bad. There was no getting around the fact that some people would have a hard time listing positive lessons from their dads. But, as I told my readers, acknowledging the bad stuff means you have learned something from your father, albeit the hard way. There was only one response to that point: "My dad taught me how not to be a father. If I could do everything completely opposite, my son may be president one day."

The rest of the reader responses were overwhelmingly positive, full of gratitude and love. Men and women from all over, most of them baby boomers, took the opportunity to write sweet tributes and to enumerate things their dads had said or taught them. Here are a few:

- "Intelligent people don't have to cuss to express themselves."

- "Don't quit a job because of the other guy; he may drop dead the next day."

- "Only drink beer; it has water in it, keeps you cleaned out, and you won't get stones."

- "Always wear an undershirt; you are not well-dressed without one."

- "My father taught me the Our Father. He taught me to pray."

- "He taught me to give a firm handshake while looking the other party in the eye."

- "He taught me to never pick on someone or fight someone weaker than me."

- "My father began my sense of race consciousness and pride. We'd watch baseball and boxing together. I would root for Muhammad Ali and he would root for anyone who fought Ali. But while watching baseball, he would say around the time of the All-Star game in those days, 'Root for the National League, son, they got more Negro ballplayers.'"

- "My dad insisted that my sisters and brother and I stick together. We do. We may fuss with each other from time to time, but don't mess with any one of us or you'll have to mess with us all. I always told my two daughters to stick together, when they were coming along. Through thick and thin, they do."

- "My father taught me how to swim, how to eat crabs, how to enjoy friends, that you should never leave a ballgame early no matter how bad things look, and that you should stay away from golf if you can't break 100."

- "Always tell the truth; it hurts less than getting caught in a lie."

- "Always smile; it makes people wonder what you're up to."

- "You are smart enough to do whatever you want, if you take the time to figure it out."

- "'Every jackass thinks his load is the heaviest' was my father's response whenever I complained about having to do more work than my younger sisters and brother. I hear his voice in my head. You can bet I think twice before I complain about anything."

- "My father was from Nebraska, and he taught me how to drive in the snow when I was 16."

- "When in a snowball fight, make the largest, most-packed snowball you can throw so that when you hit your buddies, it will put the fear of God in them, lessening the chances that they will ambush you at a later time."

- "My meshugana daddy taught me to love and revere old buildings, to be self-sufficient in case something happened to him (it did), to promote a cause (or myself) with humor and style, to be a Renaissance woman, and he taught me (inadvertently) that life is short, so have as much fun as possible."

- "Get a good liberal arts education."

- "If you miss your exit, don't back up on the freeway."

- "My father taught me how to tuck a shirt in. Every Sunday before Mass he'd make sure I was presentable. He taught me how to tie a Windsor knot. Most importantly, my father taught me through example to be fair and beyond reproach in business and life."

- "The most memorable thing my father taught me was: 'There's always room for ice cream. It slides right down.' It's become a family mantra. We've taught our children this lesson as well."

- "My father taught me to drive with a manual transmission, which I still think is the coolest skill in the world. I consider a manual transmission the best theft deterrent there is."

- "My father taught me that doing the simplest things with your children (finger tricks, sharing mementos in your desk drawer, flying a kite, reading together, putting rubber bands around an empty tissue box in the hospital so I could make music) helps develop a strong relationship and warm memories."

- "When I was about 19 years old, my father said, 'What you have done up to now reflects on me; what you do from now on reflects on you.' He was a man of few words, but he chose them well."

- "When I was in the second grade, my dad helped me build a lemonade stand and taught me about profits and inventory costs. Until then, I hadn't even thought about paying for lemons, sugar, cups and stuff. Later that summer we opened a bank account, and he taught me how to balance a checkbook. He also taught me how to say 'Yes, sir,' and 'Yes, ma'am.' God bless him."

- "Even back in the 'olden days' of the '40s and '50s, I was never told that I couldn't do something because I was a girl. So I've never been afraid to try anything that I wanted to try, and have enjoyed a lot of happiness and success as a result."

- "My father taught me to believe in humanity. There was never anyone above or below him in the hierarchy of the human race, and he tried by his example to make sure that I took that belief into my future. He taught me the rewards of love, tenacity, patience, suffering and service."

- "He taught me that life was never easy, but that it was

always rewarding, if you lived it to your best."

- "My father taught me how to say, 'I love you.' I grew up in a family where we didn't express our love for each other outwardly. Then, all of a sudden after I left home for college, my father started ending all of our conversations with 'I love you.' Now, every time I talk to my father or another family member, I always end the conversation with 'I love you.'"

Among the many old black-and-white movies that appeared on the television in my boyhood home were Andy Hardy stories, a series of sappy comedies from the 1930s and 1940s starring a young Mickey Rooney as Andy and an old Lewis Stone as his father. The plots of these movies followed basically the same line: Andy would get in trouble in some way, or he would lie about something, then he would end up having a heart-to-heart with his dad, a wise-in-all-things judge who looked more grandfatherly than fatherly. After a pow-wow in Judge Hardy's den, Andy went out and did the right thing. I found this model of the father-son relationship ideal: Dad as oracle in a wing chair; all a boy had to do was ask for help, and help would be delivered in a firm, kind and wise way. Dad's solution would be impeccable, too. It would be logical and moral, and relatively easy to execute.

That was not what came out of transactions with my father. I can think of only one time when Joe Rodricks pulled me aside to give some direct, unsolicited advice, and that was when he suspected I had lied about the reason to be out late one night in my sophomore year of high school. Instead of getting angry, as he usually did, and accusing me of lying, as he often did, he decided to provide a tempered warning about girls and how "even the nice ones" could get a boy in trouble. He nervously delivered the brief lecture – more like an admonition – while I pulled weeds in the garden, then went about his business. That is as close as we came to an Andy Hardy-Judge Hardy moment.

Most of my father's life lessons, if they could be called that, occurred during a storm of anger. He did not have conversations. He had eruptions. He died in 1986, and, of course, I said none of this in delivering the eulogy at his funeral. I spoke only of my father's good qualities – his hardcore work ethic, his skills at gardening, and his calloused hands as proof of a productive life. But, for me, his legacy includes a lesson in how to be an effective father, and the lesson is straightforward: Do not be like Iron Joe. Emulate his best traits, avoid his worst. I look at his photo and remember the times we went fishing together as well as the times he yelled and brought a belt to my ass. My advice to young men who had rough relations with dad: Remember all of it. But take only the good with you when it's your turn to be a father. It's hard, but you can do it.

When my wife was pregnant with our son, she read a lot of books on caring for babies and raising children. But none of the advice she ever shared with me was as effective as her reminders about my father – specifically, when I spoke and behaved like Iron Joe. If I raised my voice, if I lost control and slipped into anger, she would simply say, "OK, *Joe,*" and I would re-enter Earth's normal atmosphere. I would remember my resolve.

I am no expert on this, by any means, but I think I can say this much: Effective fatherhood does not just happen. It takes work. And communicating well with your son or daughter takes training. If you grew up with a father whose idea of effective parenting involved anger, a lot of yelling and spanking, you need to envision a model that includes none of those things.

The Andy Hardy-Judge Hardy model might be a Hollywood fantasy, but there is no harm in holding it as an ideal.

There is a lot of talk about what fatherhood cannot be because of the nature of fatherhood – the idea that the relationship between dads and their kids, especially their sons, is fraught and volatile, or too fragile to be tested too much. I have heard it said that a father cannot be a friend to his children, that the job requires the father to be emotionally aloof so that he can nurture the child with objective wisdom and a strong hand. These arguments make fatherhood sound inherently awful, totally problematic from the date of birth.

It does not have to be that way. I claim no perfection, in either fatherhood or fly fishing, but I have worked at both and attained a certain level of competency. I do not fish as my father fished. I do not father as he did, either. My children still speak to me. I consider this progress, and in just one generation, pretty damn good.

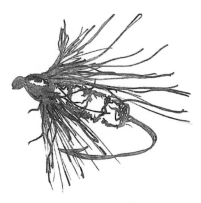

Because of a recent rainfall, the water in Father's Day Creek was about a half-foot higher than normal. The section I intended to fish is usually shallow enough that you can successfully prospect for trout with an attractor pattern – a larger-than-life dry fly that does not match the hatch, per se, but looks enticing enough to get the fish excited. However, on this day, because of the higher flow, and because I wanted to catch one more trout before breakfast, I decided to switch to a nymph imitation – that is, a fly that imitates one of the creek's aquatic insects in its nymphal stage. It does not float on the surface; it should look as though it is swimming through the water column, and pretty close to the bottom. I selected a prince nymph, a beauty I had obtained with a donation to Trout Unlimited. I stepped carefully into the stream at a spot where it is only about 30 feet wide. In that moment, it occurred to me that I know all the fishy places along a mile of the creek. As I stood there, tying the nymph to the tippet, I had the fanciful thought of living out the rest of my life in a small hut with a Franklin stove along the banks of Father's Day Creek, asking everyone who comes there to fish it gently – fool the fish, land them, let them go. I finished tying the fly to the tippet. It was time to make another cast.

Some fathers think they should be Super Dads – patriarch, protector, provider, guidance counselor, teacher, scold and an expert on just about everything, from changing a tire to saving a marriage. But fathers do not need to do it all. In fact, they can't. They must defer some of the male-side nurturing of their children to other men – coaches and teachers, maybe a summer boss or clergyman who play smaller but influential roles as boys and girls grow up.

"The old male initiators – King Arthur was one – are interested in the souls of the young man," the poet Robert Bly wrote. "That's what the young men are missing, that there aren't any older men who are interested in their souls."

They do not make Father's Day cards for what Bly called the old male initiators, our fathers who are not our fathers. In his orations at gatherings of men, Bly called these elders "the male mothers." There is no day set aside to honor them. And yet, they deserve honor.

When I first heard Bly speak of old male initiators, I knew what he meant – those men who could offer a boy instruction in the rites of manhood that a father could not. But that romantic idea of elders being interested in our souls – *our souls?* – threw me off, and I spent several years thinking about it. Bly's men's movement, famous for the ritualistic beating of drums during male gatherings, might have deserved some of the ridicule it received. And the feminist critique – that the movement was a celebration of masculinity and patriarchy – made me self-conscious about talking Bly talk in public. But, as the years went by and I reflected on the poet's insights about the human soul and about American society, I found them keen. The men who poked fun at Bly's gatherings probably needed to attend one.

Bly's ideas about what he saw as a hole in the soul of modern men went back to the Industrial Revolution, which removed many fathers from their households and from the company of their sons, leaving voids to be filled by what Bly called the "male mothers." These older men saw in young men the future of the world, not merely the future of commerce. They sought to instill virtue and integrity by word, deed and example. They were stewards of the principled life.

You will have to attach your own names and faces to the men who fit this description. Looking back, I can think of more than a dozen men I should honor on Father's Day, for each made a contribution, each performed the beautiful deed of taking an interest in me and the kind of person I might turn out to be. They encouraged me. I count Jay, Gene, Ernie, Ed, Fred, Gordie, Jack, Al, Dave, Tom, Vince, Carl, Gil, Chris and Bill. I can see their faces and recall the lessons they taught. To each name I can attach a specific virtue they shared by word, deed and example: Jay, creativity and common sense; Gene, humor, generosity and service to others; Ernie and Ed and Fred, craftsmanship, vigilance, integrity and persistence; Gordie and Jack, hard work and teamwork; Dave, daring to be great, resisting self-imposed limitations; Al, leadership and discipline; Tom, blunt honesty and self-reflection; Vince, the importance of praising others, especially the young, for the good they do; Carl, the beauty of words, art, craft and humanity; Gil, the power of story and the importance of encouraging young people; Chris, conscience, sacrifice and devotion to others; Bill, love of the outdoors and the gift of friendship.

Robert Bly, fully licensed as a poet and sage, uses Arthur, a mythical character, as his first model. Here was a king interested in the souls of young men – what they believed, how they treated others, the decisions they made under pressure – and he offered to be their mentor. There was a time, Bly noted, when young men would travel hundreds of miles to find a mentor to provide the emotional nourishment, experience and wisdom that did not come from their fathers. Indeed, it could only come freely from a man who was not the father. Most memorable among Bly's teachings was one he picked up from the late psychoanalyst Robert Moore: "If you are a young man and you're not being admired by an older man, you're being hurt." Bly presented that to older men as a responsibility, recognizing that boys and young men still need the acceptance of their elders. The elders have forgotten to provide it, Bly claimed, and the young men have not learned to ask for it. In earlier times, in extended families, there were uncles to serve as "male mothers." Or there was a grandfather, maybe two, and perhaps a grandfather's friend. If a boy could not reach his father – if the father was physically or emotionally distant or absent – another man could stand in.

By the late 20th Century, Bly lamented that such relationships no longer existed, or that they were too rare for the good of society. My contribution to that hypothesis has to do with the loss of small-town America, the decline of city neighborhoods after white flight, the spread of suburbia and its isolated nature. As more and more Americans moved away from the old industrial centers of the East, going West and Southwest for sun and careers, they lost touch with their extended families. Men broke further away from their fathers – as either something desired or forced by divorce – but they also lost regular contact with the wider circle of "male mothers."

So I look at those dynamics and tend to agree with Bly. Less contact with the old initiators and "male mothers" might explain, in part, why the 1980s were regarded as the Get-Mine, Every-Man-For-Himself years. Throughout the turbulent, divisive period of the Vietnam War and through the Reagan presidency, there were not enough older men interested in the souls of young men, and a major cultural change occurred, almost completely undetected. There are many ways to measure the decline of a society. Bly's was one of the more profound and logical, and the logic led to his second major thesis, what he called a "sibling society," a nation of half-adults obsessed with consumerism and pop culture, demanding quick pleasures and excitements. In this adolescent culture, empathy for children and respect for elders disappear. Social and political leaders strive not to be good, or great, but to be famous. Voters become disillusioned. Young men, who search instinctively for role models, cannot locate enough genuine grownups and end up in protracted, self-centered adolescence – all to the detriment of American society. As I write this, Donald J. Trump is president of the United States, and so, with that tragic development, Robert Bly, poet and mystic, earns the title of prophet.

I cast the prince nymph to five or six different spots below the plunge pool in Father's Day Creek, striving to make it drift naturally through the water column in the same way I want my dry flies to drift on the surface. You want the drift to be as natural as possible, soft and steady. You don't want the fly to "motorboat" through the water. I am not very patient with nymphs. I do not fish them as often as I do dry flies, and that's because the dry fly fishing is so visual and exciting; you see the rise and the take. Nymphing is a generally more productive form of fly fishing because, most of the time, nymphs are what trout are looking for in the depths of pools. But I had no hookups. My mind drifted to my father-in-law's galettes, with maybe some of that delicious thick-cut bacon he gets from the butcher up the road. I decided it was time for The One More – one more spot and one more cast on Father's Day.

The death of Edward Querzoli, when he was 68 and I was 46, made me realize that my male mentors were disappearing. (My female mentors seem to live a lot longer.) One by one, I lost those older men who leaned on the outfield fences of my life to tell me how to play just about any ball that came my way. Though their influence endures, I sense from their deaths an emptiness in the psychic spaces they inhabited.

Ed was my first newspaper editor, and his teachings about reporting news stayed with me long past the time I worked for him. He was always there, in some way, always looking over his apprentice's shoulder.

Ed was survived by his wife, his 13 children and 24 grandchildren. His funeral was in the Roman Catholic church by the cemetery where my father is buried. On the occasion of Querzoli's passing, I took inventory of the old "male mothers," the ones who were generous with their time, who taught the value of hard work and honesty. They advocated common sense over foolishness, generosity over greed, enduring friendships over the desire to be liked by everyone, integrity over everything else. They shared a lot of what they had learned in life. My mentors could give direct advice, when asked, but their teaching was mostly situational, and by example. They challenged me to think hard about what I was doing and to push myself. I was lucky to have known them. I wish I had known some of them a lot longer.

These thoughts occurred to me one day while on assignment for *The Sun*. I sat next to police officers in a small room in the Clarence M. Mitchell Jr. Courthouse in downtown Baltimore. A boy, whose first 15 years of life could not have been more different from mine, sat at the trial table as men and women in the room decided what to do with him.

The boy's father was not part of his life. His mother had been in jail for many years. The boy lived with his grandmother. Many of the male figures around him were involved in drug dealing; one of them, a man known as Mackey, had been recently killed. The boy wound up in Juvenile Court, charged with possession and distribution of cocaine, after a police officer caught him holding cocaine one winter day on Pennsylvania Avenue in West Baltimore. The boy had skipped school 100 times because he could make $200 to $300 a day in the drug market.

Now he was in court, dressed in a sweatshirt and jeans, awaiting "disposition." He was one of the thousands of kids who grow up the hard way, in poor neighborhoods infested with drugs, and who find in the entrepreneurial cool of the drug dealer a role model. In court, the boy was silent and glum, maybe a little frightened.

The public defender wanted him to get probation and go home with his grandmother. But the prosecutor and staff of juvenile services wanted the boy to spend about six months in a supervised group home.

His grandmother, a stout woman with a stack of curls on her head and large-frame eyeglasses, came to court to ask for help. The boy had lived with her since he was 6 months old, and in recent years he had been a lot of trouble, she said. He had joined some friends on a television-stealing caper in a Baltimore suburb. He had constantly violated his 9 o'clock weeknight curfew. He had violated his 11 o'clock Saturday night curfew, too. The boy had been hanging with bad guys, the grandmother said.

"This is why I came here, to get help," she told Zakia Mahasa, a juvenile court master. "I have seen too many young people in my neighborhood end up six feet under."

Then Mahasa asked the boy what he wanted, and the boy stood at the trial table and, in a quiet voice with a minor tremble, said: "I'd like to stay home. I want a chance to get some help. I ain't had no chance to get no help. I want to get back in school."

"Who put a gun to your head and told you to go sell drugs on the corner?" Mahasa asked. "What was that friend's name?"

"Mackey," the grandmother answered.

"You were out on probation," Mahasa said, "and two days later you were out on Pennsylvania Avenue. You went and possessed drugs because you wanted to. Take responsibility for your own actions. That's life."

Mahasa's eyes dropped to a report. "You have potential, it says here. What do you want to be when you grow up?"

"A basketball player."

There was little chance of that, Mahasa said. "What's Plan B?"

"Bricklayer."

Mahasa told the boy he would never learn to be a bricklayer by hanging out on the streets. He was a cute little boy once, and now he was a handsome young man. But, without changing his life, he could end up like his role model, Mackey, and people from his neighborhood will be glad he's gone.

"Do you want to be one of those that people say, 'Glad he's gone?'" Mahasa asked. Did the boy want to spend his life in prison?

Mahasa decided to send the boy to a group home. That would get him away from Pennsylvania Avenue for a while. "This might be a chance to turn it around," she told him. "This is not a punishment. It's a chance to turn it around."

A clerk banged at a computer keyboard. A juvenile officer snapped handcuffs around the boy's wrists. He puts shackles around his ankles, above the boy's white crew socks and sneakers, and walked him out of the room.

The prosecutor that day was a fellow named Steve Mitchell. He told me the case was typical in many ways. "For one thing, his grandmother was there," Mitchell said. "We see that a lot. His grandmother is there because she doesn't want to see the child die."

The grandmother was unable to get the boy away from Pennsylvania Avenue. This happened a lot, especially in the many single-parent, or single-grand-parent, households throughout the city. Little boys become bigger boys and slip under the influence of men who hire them as lookouts on drug corners.

But Baltimore is not one vast, dysfunctional inner-city family in denial about this problem. For decades there has been great frustration over the number of boys who are recruited into the violent drug culture, and there have been efforts to address it. "The overwhelming majority of parents and grandparents, aunts and uncles and neighbors of these kids care what's going on and want help for them," Mitchell told me. "They want to keep their kids out of it. They really do."

As an assistant state's attorney in Baltimore, Mitchell had started in the juvenile division, transferred to other prosecution units, then shocked his supervisor by asking to return to juvenile court.

"This unit is the most important one in the state's attorney's office," he said. "I could do jury trials. That's what prosecutors think we all went to law school for. I can prosecute a 25-year-old for armed robbery, but he's an adult and by then he's unlikely to change. They get into that gangsta lifestyle early because it's what they see and what they think is cool. We have to get to them before that becomes their mindset."

That's why Mitchell returned to the juvenile division, and there were many days when he wished he had had more time to personally mentor more of the boys he saw at the trial table. He and some friends had been doing exactly that for several years, treating boys to experiences they otherwise would never have had, emphasizing the importance of education, telling stories that might help them make smart decisions. The smartest, and hardest, decision Mitchell ever made was when he was 15 and growing up on Chicago's South Side. He not only refused to join a gang that roamed his neighborhood, but he resisted the urgings of friends to retaliate against a gang member who had shot and wounded him with a .22-caliber handgun. "If I had retaliated," Mitchell said, "I would probably not be here today."

A year later, he made another smart decision.

"I had a buddy who cut my hair in Chicago. And one day he rode up on me on the street and asked did I want to ride with him on an armed robbery. He just wanted someone to come along with him, and I could have half the money. And I said no. And do you know I didn't see him for eight years? He went away for that long, and I was mad because me and him were cool, and he was the only one who cut my hair right. But I tell this story to kids. I can't tell you why I didn't get in that car. I could say it was a complex decision-making process, but it wasn't. I just made the right decision."

Mitchell was not the only one involved in that decision. Others had helped, long before the moment arrived. He had a mentor named Harold Washington, a Chicago congressman who took an interest in him when Mitchell was in high school. Washington had given him an interview for a term paper. Later, Washington became Chicago's first black mayor, and Mitchell worked in his political campaigns and stayed in touch with him. "He saw potential in me, and he said he expected me to succeed," Mitchell said. "He was tough. He wouldn't accept failure." He took an interest in Mitchell's soul.

Washington died in 1987, but the influence he had on Steve Mitchell endures. We all mourn the loss of our old and honorable mentors. But sit in Baltimore Juvenile Court for an hour and you'll feel much deeper grief for all the boys who never had them at all.

For The One More I chose a fishy-looking run about 50 yards upstream of the bridge. I pinched some clinging algae off my prince nymph and dropped it into the stream above a subtle riffle and let it drift downstream with the current. It sank slowly. I held the rod over the river with my right hand and held the yellow fly line steady with my left, careful to take up any slack. Suddenly the line stopped. Had I snagged bottom? Perhaps the run was not as deep as I had thought. If it was a snag, I would know in a moment and, if so, I would reel in the line and call it a day. I had caught enough trout. I was happy. I felt good about the creek. A snag would mean it was time for breakfast. But when I tugged on the line, something tugged back, and that something started swimming away from me.

Fly-fishing involves a lot of thinking about fish and their habitat, and many dismiss it as arcane, too expensive and too much trouble. The attempt to precisely and delicately cast a tiny artificial fly that imitates the size, shape and movement of the insects that trout crave is a challenge. The process looks to bait fishermen – keepers of my father's way of fishing – like a lot of work for little reward. *"All that for that?"*

But one can get lost in the challenge, the geometry of the cast, the attempt to drop a fly on the current for a few pregnant seconds in the hopes of deceiving a wild trout. You want the trout to see the fly coming, recognize it as food, rise to the surface and attack it. They are exquisite little creatures, and they spend a moment in your net or hand before returning to the water and their holding spots.

Mike Flanagan was really good at this kind of fishing, much better than I was. I never got to take Mike to Father's Day Creek, and that regret lives like a sullen ghost in the wells of my conscience. Things would have been better had we fished together more, I am certain of it, and Mike would have loved Father's Day Creek, though parts of it might have been a challenge for a retired pitcher who cast with his left hand.

So here is where I tell you how I gained and lost a friend.

I was host of an evening radio show on WBAL in Baltimore from 1989 to 1993, and during that time contributed some recorded essays and live reports to the station's coverage of the Baltimore Orioles and

Major League Baseball. Until then, I had only spent a few days around the team – when the Orioles won the World Series in 1983, when the hapless 1988 team lost the first 21 games of the season (and 86 more after that), when the 1989 "Why Not?" team chased the Blue Jays for the Eastern Division championship of the American League into the final weekend of the season in Toronto. Two years later, the Orioles played their final season at Memorial Stadium, on the north side of Baltimore. A couple of generations of Baltimoreans had extracted gallons of sweet memories from that place. It was home, from 1953 until 1983, of the storied Colts of the National Football League, and of the Orioles from the moment the franchise moved to Baltimore from St. Louis in 1954. As part of the radio station's coverage of the final season at Memorial Stadium, I conducted live interviews on the field on Opening Day in April 1991. I was standing by the third base line when Mike Flanagan walked by in his uniform, a black-and-orange jacket over his left shoulder. He said a quick hello and shook my hand. That was the first time I met him. I had been an admirer from a distance, having watched him from the stands. At that point, I knew him only as a left-handed pitcher, and not as a fly fisherman.

Mike was the Cy Young Award winner of 1979, the year the Orioles won 102 games and their fifth American League pennant. It was the year of "Orioles Magic," and no prior season had been as exhilarating. Even when the Orioles won earlier pennants, attendance at Memorial Stadium had been mediocre. As I was growing up in Massachusetts in the 1960s and early 1970s, I watched most Red Sox games on television, and I was always bewildered by camera shots of empty stands when the Sox played the Orioles in Baltimore. "It's a football town," my father explained.

But something happened in 1979. It was as if the entire Baltimore region, as well as fans from the District of Columbia, had suddenly become smitten with baseball and Earl Weaver's Orioles. Attendance started to climb, the team won a number of important games in dramatic fashion, and people started calling it "Orioles Magic." Mike Flanagan was in the middle of all that excitement, the longhaired lefty and ace of an excellent rotation of starters that included Jim Palmer, Steve Stone, Scott McGregor and Dennis Martinez.

Mike pitched for the Orioles from 1975 to 1987. He went to the Blue Jays for a few years, then returned to the Orioles as a reliever for the 1991 season, the last at Memorial Stadium. Mike was good. He was steady. He was smart. He fooled many of the 11,684 batters he faced over 18 big league seasons. He won 167 games, striking out nearly 1,500 batters in the process. On Oct. 6, 1991, the Orioles played their last game at Memorial Stadium, losing to Detroit. Mike, then 39 years old, came in from the bullpen in the top of the ninth inning and shut down the Tigers. It was a beautiful moment. He struck out the last two batters he faced. I watched from the press box as Mike left the field to a prolonged ovation from an emotional and nostalgic crowd. In the long shadows of that autumn afternoon, Mike lifted his head, raised his black cap and wiped a tear from his eye.

His last appearance for the Orioles was in September 1992, in the new ballpark at Camden Yards. But, unlike most of his old teammates, he did not leave town. Mike loved the game and the Orioles, and it was his hope to stay involved in the organization.

The following year, while I was on the air and taking calls from listeners, Mike's wife encouraged him to phone into my radio show from his car. He said he had heard I liked fly fishing and suggested we get together, and the whole thing was pretty cool – a Cy Young Award winner and Orioles Hall of Famer inviting me to go fishing with him while thousands of people listened on WBAL.

And so we met and started fishing together, first in home waters around Baltimore and then later in western Maryland. He was a great companion and conversationalist, always in good humor. We became friends after most of his old teammates and fishing buddies from the glory years of the Orioles had scattered across the country. We were transplanted New Englanders, rooted in Maryland and approaching middle age with fly rods in our hands — mine in my right, Mike's in his left. Because he was a southpaw, we could wade to the middle of a river — the Big Gunpowder Falls in Baltimore County or the Youghiogheny River in western Maryland — and stand side-by-side and cast to separate banks. It was a good system, though one time I managed to hook a caddis fly in Mike's neck on my back-cast, something neither he nor I noticed until hours later when he asked his wife to remove what he thought was a tick. Fortunately, the barbless hook made the extraction simple, and I got my fly back.

Mike always managed to catch more trout on the left bank than I did on the right, but he never rubbed that in, and he never bragged. He just loved the visual experience of seeing a trout rise to his fly. His ability to catch wild trout was uncanny. While I practiced the craft of fly fishing as it had been taught to me, trying to match the flies that hatched in the river with the manmade feather-and-fur ones in my fly box, Mike eschewed the science and caught three times the fish I did with just about any old fly that would float and that looked right in the moment. He was blessed with great eyesight — "Ted Williams' eyes," I called them — and he could spot trout, make perfect casts to them and instill the lightest, magical charge into the line to make a fly flicker and dance, tantalizing trout looking for a meal.

We fished the Gunpowder at a time when that river's reputation as a trout stream was spreading throughout the East. One late-spring afternoon, Mike quietly caught a half dozen trout, one after another, as visiting anglers from other states, who had been skunked in their daylong efforts, watched in disbelief.

We fished in Pennsylvania and in New York. We made several trips with one of Mike's best friends, the Orioles longtime trainer Richie Bancells, to the healthy rivers of western Maryland. We had a memorable day on Deer Creek in Harford County, during an April shad run, when we stood side by side and landed and released 100 fish between us.

We also fished the creek that flowed through Mike's land in Sparks, north of Baltimore. It was in 1998, a few days before Thanksgiving, when we went prospecting in the creek for the first time. By then, Mike had been busy with the Orioles, serving in different capacities – pitching coach, scout, broadcaster – and he had not had time to survey the creek on his property. Our expectations were low. But we found wild trout and caught a fat, 14-inch brown in his bold autumn courting colors, and if there was ever a moment of male bonding over a discovery, that was it. We felt like Lewis and Clark.

So we fished his creek often over the years, driving in Mike's John Deere gator to a fence line, and then traipsing through the woods to the water. We didn't talk about the Orioles unless Mike wanted to. I did not think it was my place to talk shop with him. Our fishing together was a break from all that. After the 1997 season, when the team had won the Eastern Division but lost in the playoffs to Cleveland, the franchise experienced a lot of losing, a lot of frustration. Season after season. Mike took on more responsibility; he worked harder and harder, and we didn't fish as much as we should have. He loved Baltimore and wanted to restore the Orioles to the winning ways he had known in the 1970s and 1980s.

But, as time went on, we talked less and less about fishing and more about his frustrations, and I heard in his voice something I had never heard in the two decades of our friendship – bitterness. When he lost his job as the Orioles' vice president for baseball operations, he felt kicked aside and wholly unappreciated. He asked me about writing a book together, a tell-all about the demise of a great baseball franchise. At first, I was not sure he was serious. But, during a second conversation, it was clear that Mike believed his days in the Orioles organization were over, and he really wanted to write such a book. Some time after that, in early 2010, he signed on as a TV color commentator again. Though he desired a greater role with the club, I thought Mike was getting his groove back, and by the summer of 2011, I assumed that we would go fishing again in October, when the season ended. That was our routine — baseball and business in spring and summer, fishing and replenished friendship in the fall and early winter.

I spoke to Mike of making a trip to Father's Day Creek. I really wanted to share it with him, just as he had shared with me the creek behind his house. But we never got there. I did not stay in touch with Mike as the summer of 2011 progressed. I was busy, by then serving as host of a public radio show while still writing columns for the *Sun*. The compensation from those jobs allowed me to get my son and daughter through college, but the schedule of work deprived me of fishing time with a friend who apparently needed it more than I did.

On Aug. 24, Mike killed himself with a shotgun blast on the grounds of his stone farmhouse, on a spot above the creek we had fished together. He was 59 years old.

When I heard the news late that night, I felt shock and heartbreak, confusion, an awful, searing sense of loss – and guilt that we had not been together in months. I knew Mike had been frustrated with the Orioles, and that he had grown bitter about his situation in the front office. But I thought his distress had been relieved by the return to broadcasting. It had not. And Mike kept secrets. He had not let on that mid-life depression – what Howell Raines called "the black dog" in his book on fly fishing – was still following him, deep in the dark forest. Either he had not called out for help or we had not heard him, and I will wonder about that for the rest of my life.

Mike had had financial pressures from a lapse of steady income between jobs with the Orioles. That caused him to dip deeply into savings and into his player pension, and to inquire about his life insurance policy. Those issues trickled out after Mike's death as we looked for an explanation. Money pressures made some sense, I guess, but they seemed too simple. Mike was depressed, and for a long time, and deeper than any of his friends knew, including me. "Most people won't believe it, but I don't think Mike ever believed in himself," Alex, his wife, later told me. Despite all his accomplishments, she said, Mike suffered from low self-esteem. He had trouble accepting his success. "He felt . . . he had just been lucky," she said. "He was self-effacing in his humor, and that was part of his charm. But that was a cover for insecurity."

In all the times I went fishing with him, Mike rarely opened up about problems, and I never pried. He would sometimes briefly vent about trying to make the Orioles a winning franchise again. He shared unhappiness about his status in the organization after his stint as vice president. He spoke of young pitchers who did not listen to his advice and called him "dude." Mike was heart and soul an Oriole, a believer in what was known as the Oriole Way. He worked long hours trying to turn the franchise around. But he was disillusioned by the modern baseball business, and the Orioles' streak of 13 losing seasons affected him more than I ever realized. There were a lot of cruel statements made by fans on Internet forums, and Mike apparently read many of them, and they brought him great pain.

I always found Mike affable and funny, endlessly telling stories about his teammates from the 1970s and 1980s and about their excitable manager, Earl Weaver. And he was really focused on catching trout. He never mentioned money problems or having been treated by a psychiatrist. He drank plenty of Scotch on our fishing trips, but I never saw him drunk. On overnight trips to western Maryland, he would fall asleep and be up early the next day, looking for coffee, eager to get back to the river.

People who knew Mike wonder how we missed seeing pain so severe he would take his own life and leave people he loved in so much grief and anguish. He was intelligent and witty. The sportswriter Buster Olney called him the funniest man in baseball. Mike wrote comic poems, appreciated all kinds of music, and loved the outdoors. He long ago earned the respect of thousands of fans around Baltimore who remembered Orioles Magic. The following generation, my kids, knew him as a competent television broadcaster, knowledgeable baseball man and a generally pleasant guy who was quick with a quip or a silly pun. He was good at a lot of things, especially, it's clear, at hiding his anguish. Mike had a stoic New England streak in him, and I guess it disguised his depression.

I have guessed at a lot of things since we lost him in the dark forest.

The black dog chased me once, for about four years, when I was in my early 30s. The depression was so surprisingly severe – incapacitating at times – that it still scares me just to think about it. I had help. I had support. I survived. I moved on, ever watchful for the black dog's reappearance. Having children gave my life more significance and meaning. Seeing them grow up, leave home and become independent makes me melancholy at times. Seeing your old friends get sick and die will do that, too. But middle-aged melancholy is just a mild itch compared to the awful, confusing, debilitating pain of deep depression. I emerged scarred but unbroken. I still carry the memory of those dark days, something like a phantom pain, as a reminder of life's fragility, of how easy it is to stumble and fall – and how absolutely wonderful it is to leave the forest and find your way into sunlight.

I never got a chance to share any of my insights about depression with Flanny. He never asked for them, and I never appreciated his pain as anything more than temporary frustration over his status with a baseball franchise. And so my regret – my guilt – comes from having missed his signals. It comes from surviving depression but failing to recognize it in my friend with the fly rod, the guy standing next to me in the river. It comes from taking our friendship for granted, assuming that it could not be damaged by neglect, that it would always be there, until we were too old to tie fly to tippet. We should have fished more, and I should have taken him to Pennsylvania and exposed him to the healing powers of Father's Day Creek.

You will have to trust me here. I know this will sound too good, or overly dramatic, or even cinematic. But I realized I had hooked a nice fish, so I knew I had to savor the moment in vivid detail. My senses were on full alert, and I tell you this with full certainty: Like a moment from Arthurian legend, sunlight fell through the gloomy hemlocks and hit the water precisely on the spot where this trout tried to shake the fly from its lip. And so I could see the silver flash, clear as Excalibur.

I had hooked a rainbow trout.

A large one.

By far the largest fish I had ever hooked in Father's Day Creek.

The rainbow swam hard behind a rock and held there until I could gently but firmly pull him away. He made another run, and I kept the line tight. I imagined my father was watching, as he did back in the deep-sea days aboard the Nan-Sue, smiling and laughing as I pulled in the catch: "Don't stop. Keep it comin'." I could sense the rainbow finally coming my way, so I took up the slack. Then I reached for my net. I was in mild shock as I squatted and scooped this exquisite fish out of the river. The net could hardly contain him. The trout seemed too big to be true, out of scale with the 20-foot wide section of water in which I had found him. I wanted to scream.

Sometime, as when the fishing stinks or when the whole world seems cloudy and ominous, I like to stand peaceably by a river, throw the dead branch of a tree in the current and watch it go. I did this when I was a kid so that my friends downstream would have something to bombard with rocks as it drifted by, and I did it as a dad for my kids – we called the game "Bombs Away" – and I do it when I hike or fish alone now. I do it for the same reason some people call psychic hot lines – to see how the future might go.

I know that sounds weird. But it's what I do. I take a moment at the end of a fishing day on Father's Day Creek and I drop a good-size stick into the current, then try to keep my eyes on it as it floats downstream. If the branch flows freely all the way to some goal I've set with my eye – a bridge, a leaning sycamore or an old fence post 30 yards away – then I take that as a sign that things will go well in the next year, or at least the next few days. If, instead, the branch gets hung up on a rock or in some brush, then maybe not. Maybe I lay low. Maybe I avoid risks.

There is an art to this driftin'-stick game. You can't just toss the stick into the water and hope for the best. You have to study the stream and find the ribbon of current that will take it – and you – the farthest.

I did this one New Year's Day, during a hike on a rainy, soppy, foggy afternoon along the creek on Mike Flanagan's snow-covered farm.

The creek was a crooked little thing, but full of water from the rain and melting snow. In fact, I had never seen such a strong current in the creek. Usually the water levels are moderate to low, and during drought they get pitifully low. But on that day, the creek was back up and looking strong again.

We had started calling this place Coffee Can Creek because a truck carrying coffee tipped over and, as it crashed to the roadside, dumped some of its cargo into the water. The creek smelled like coffee for several hours. We hiked its banks and found numerous dented No. 10 cans of Maxwell House, their contents dry. We took a bunch of them home.

Coffee Can is not the best creek for my driftin'-stick ritual – too many bends, downed trees and beaver dams. It presents a challenge. But on that New Year's Day, I dropped a little Y-shaped stick, something like a divining rod, into the current and watched it until it disappeared. It went as far as I had wished it would go, and maybe farther. So I think the year got off to a promising start.

The Jewish New Year has a ritual like this, though it's not so much about assessing the future as it is about purging the past. It is Tashlich. I first witnessed the ritual one autumn afternoon along Cross Country Boulevard in northwest Baltimore, as whole families of Orthodox Jews observed their New Year with prayers by the banks of a small stream called Western Run. Tashlich is a custom derived from the words of the Hebrew prophet Micah: "And You, God, shall throw their sins into the depths of the sea."

All rivers run to the sea, so on the afternoon of the first day of Rosh Hashanah, Jews the world over go to where the currents are moving and symbolically cast their sins into the water. They recite scripture and prayer. Some turn their pockets inside out and shake them. A description of Tashlikh from the Etz Chaim Center for Jewish Studies says: "By praying at the water's edge we recall the merit of the patriarchs who overcame ever-raging floods in their pursuit of goodness and imply our wish to emulate their righteousness."

As solemn as it is, Tashlikh has become a social event, a gathering of friends and neighbors, everyone sharing in the fresh hope of the new year. As a religious exercise, Tashlikh appeals to me because it connects worship with nature – and, indeed, a part of nature absolutely vital to life on Earth. I like the concept of ever-moving rivers taking away sin and bad feelings. It's as if nature provides a watery conveyor belt of second chances for the fallible human race.

So I have appropriated Tashlikh from the Jewish New Year for my own purposes every January 1. When I drop a branch into the current, I am not just running a superstitious test on the future, I am letting go of the problems and failings of the past. It is sweet release.

I love rivers – big, wide, rolling ones and little, craggy, fickle ones. Rural ones. Urban ones. I go to them, walk near them and wade through them. Sometimes I catch fish in them. Sometimes I don't. Sometimes I stand there peaceably and watch and listen. Rivers are beautiful and resilient, quiet and steady, full of some of the tiniest, most delicate and fascinating forms of life on the planet. Even in dry periods, rivers hardly ever stop flowing, and so they renew your faith in the eternal. The idea that they could take away sin and bad thoughts had not occurred to me until I observed Jewish families gathering for Tashlikh along Western Run. It struck me as a wise use of a natural resource.

I could not believe the size of the trout. I stepped to the low bank, placed the rainbow trout on ferns and measured him against my catch-and-release net, notching a spot in its smooth wooden handle with my fingernail. (I later measured the notch at 17 and a half inches.) I then picked the rainbow up and looked him over. He was not a stocked fish from a hatchery because he had the bright colors and full dorsal fin of one that had grown up in the river. On the scale of all things in the universe, this might not seem like a big deal. But, for Father's Day Creek, it approached the amazing. I do not remember what I said, but in the next moment I spoke to the river and congratulated it on its endurance and its resilience. I thanked the river for its gift to me on Father's Day. I heard my own excited voice echo in the hemlock gorge. I held the trout for a moment so that my father, stirred by my shout, might appreciate it. This was no dinky fish. This was a beautiful wild animal that had been allowed to thrive. I leaned down and returned the fish to the water, feeling the muscle in its tail as it left my hand. He was still strong, but he did not dash away when I released him. Instead, he seemed to look back at me for an instant as he drifted slowly sideways, before straightening and darting into the dark folds of the creek.

Something else happened that day: I realized that, in my seventh year of fly fishing, I had become pretty good at it. That's not something I would go around saying out loud – I actually have a low tolerance for anglers who brag – but it is the kind of thing you get to acknowledge in a memoir. The 17-and-one-half-inch rainbow from Father's Day Creek was an event of double significance for me: It confirmed that the river could hold great trout and that I was capable of catching the largest, and presumably wisest, of them. I had learned how to select the best imitation of a fly to use in certain situations and how to cast it cleanly to the best spot for a good, drag-free drift so that the fly appears to be floating naturally on or in the water, therefore increasing the chances of deception. That is the whole idea, as it was taught to me. The task requires concentration and precision, and I surprised myself by developing and exhibiting these powers for the purpose of catching fish. I use the same combination when writing newspaper columns on tight deadlines – three hours, often less, of absolute focus on information, ideas and words – but fly fishing is far less stressful because my livelihood and professional standing do not rest on it. I never meditated much, never took a yoga class. Fly fishing is as close as I get to anything approaching a zen experience.

There was something else significant about the 17-and-one-half-inch rainbow in Father's Day Creek: I was alone that day. My father had died 14 years earlier, Uncle Ralph several years before that. And none of the men who had taught me how to fish on the fly – Wally Vait, Ric Martin, Stacy Smith – were there. I had reached a decent level of competency, but, more than that, I had graduated fully from the old bait-fishing ways and into this new arena where the angler did not kill, and where fishing could be a holistic experience. It was not about gathering food for the body but about gathering fuel for the soul, about wading through the natural world and feeling a part of it, about assuming the debt of stewardship for a place that still seemed perfect.

I came away from the creek that day feeling happy for the river, and for the whole idea of leaving a resource alone and giving it a chance to recover from decades of human use and abuse.

A few years later, on a sunny weekday afternoon in May, my son was with me on Father's Day Creek. He had just graduated from college. Our intent was to catch up on time together; we had not fished much during Nick's undergraduate years in Connecticut. We waded up through the gorge and stood there to admire it again and to see if any trout would give away their positions by rising to flies on the water. Almost immediately, I noticed three rises – *plunk, plunk, plunk* – and they were aggressive and splashy, too. Something had excited the trout in their feeding lanes. I heard more rises further upstream and saw more within the next 60 seconds less than 20 yards from where we stood.

"Look at the size of that fly," Nick said, as excited as I had ever heard him on a river, and he pointed to what I recognized immediately as a green drake in flight. Compared to other mayflies that come off the creek, the green drake is a condor. It is about the size of a small moth, but with upright wings of gaudy green. Trout go into a feeding frenzy when these flies emerge from the water or hover just above it. The green drake hatch does not last long on Father's Day Creek; it comes sporadically over a three-week period in late May or June, more some years than others. I had never before witnessed the hatch. But this time Nick and I had arrived at the right place at the right time, about 2 o'clock on a Tuesday, and the trout fed on the drakes for most of the next hour. My fishing journal shows that we took five brown trout, all of them chunky and muscular. They ate the drakes until the hatch tapered off. We released all the fish, of course. It was perfection within perfection: The best, most exciting and satisfying hour a fly angler could hope for – a proud father in the company of his son, casting big flies in the stretch of trout paradise above the gorge in the old river reborn. It is where I go when I need a peaceful thought. It is where I leave my spirit. It is how I want to remember life on Earth.

Post Script:

Remembrance of a springtime friend

On a Saturday morning in April 2012, I did what I had done each of the previous 20 springs: I drove to beautiful Darlington, in northeastern Maryland, near the Susquehanna River, parked my car near the Stafford Road Bridge, across from the old Flint Furnace, donned chest waders, set up my fly rod and stepped into Deer Creek to try and catch some shad during their annual migration.

There was a fellow already standing in the water, up to his waste, and he was casting to a pool where, in previous years, schools of hickory shad and Atlantic herring always seemed to stop during their journey. I grumbled a little because one of my favorite spots had been taken, and it wasn't even 7 o'clock yet.

I decided to hike downstream to another spot. I grunted hello as I walked by. The guy in the water answered me in a friendly way, then did something unusual – he invited me to step into the creek and fish right next to him, and as soon as he did this, he hooked a silvery shad. "I've caught 10 already," he said, the words topped off with a puff of cigar smoke.

At first I didn't believe the guy. I have fished a lot over the years and smirked at big talk from anglers who felt a need to brag. But I wasn't about to challenge the fellow in Deer Creek. He had just invited me to fish with him, after all, and before I could get in position to cast, he caught another hickory, about 16 inches long. I was an instant believer.

Some years ago, a buddy and I caught and released close to 100 shad in a day. When these migratory fish come up the Susquehanna River and swim into Deer Creek – when their numbers are big, and the water temperature is just right, and the sunlight is just right, and your cast is just right, and your fly is just right – you can have a day like that.

The fellow I met that Saturday was Steve Merkel. He said he had just picked up fly-fishing and had developed a secret weapon for shad – a small fly with a slanted, weighted head, and a sparse tail of silvery tinsel. Some of the flies were green and black, others orange and black. And they worked.

That first day, Steve and I barely moved 30 feet to fish. We cast his magic flies into the same big pool for the next couple of hours, and caught plenty of fish. I did not keep count. But Steve always did. Whenever I called or sent him a text message, he could tell me exactly how many shad and herring he had caught the evening before and the evening before that.

Some years were better for shad fishing than others, but you could always count on Steve being there in spring. He was, like the great blue herons perched on boulders, a fixture on Deer Creek.

I listed him in my phone contacts as Steve "Shad" Merkel. He was a good-natured, gregarious and generous man who loved to talk fishing and never let an opportunity for a conversation pass. He shared his flies with lots of anglers who were otherwise stumped in pursuit of the hickory shad.

Over time, I got to know about Steve, where he worked – he rebuilt Caterpillar engines for a local company – where he liked to fish, where he went on vacation. He loved being on water and was once a commercial crabber. He always mentioned his family, a brother, Chris, a sister, Carol, and his son, William.

And it was William who called me, in January 2019, with the shocking and sad news that his dad had just died from an aggressive cancer that had been diagnosed in late November, around Thanksgiving. Steve was 52. I did not know what to say to William except sorry, and sorry, and sorry again.

There are people we know most of our lives – from back in elementary school days – and some become and stay our friends forever. There are people we know for just parts of our lives, as in college or during military service; our friendships with them can be long lasting, too.

Then there are the people we meet several times, here and there, along life's journey. You might call them acquaintances. You might also call them seasonal friends – summer or springtime friends. We develop a bond with them. We look forward to seeing them, and it might only be once or twice a year, at a favorite restaurant, for instance, or at a farmer's market, at a baseball or football game, or at a conference for work, or during the annual trip to a family vacation spot, maybe at a familiar fishing hole in spring. They become, in their brief time with us, dear to us, and we miss them dearly when they're gone.

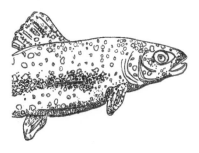

About the Author

Dan Rodricks is an award-winning columnist for *The Baltimore Sun*, and, over a journalism career spanning five decades, he has been the host of local and regional radio and television shows as well as The Sun's podcast, Roughly Speaking. His column, launched in *The Baltimore Evening Sun* in 1979, is one of the longest-running in the U.S. and has garnered regional and national journalism awards. Over the course of writing some 6,000 columns, and in his broadcasting work, Rodricks from time to time revealed his love of nature and interest in environmental issues. Excerpts of some of his outdoors columns appear in *Fathers' Day Creek*. Rodricks lives in Baltimore and has been fishing with a fly rod for nearly 30 years. He won a national broadcasting award for a radio documentary about his home waters, the Gunpowder River, north of Baltimore. He has fished extensively in western Maryland and Pennsylvania, and in the Chesapeake Bay.

Apprentice
House Press
Loyola University Maryland

Apprentice House is the country's only campus-based, student-staffed book publishing company. Directed by professors and industry professionals, it is a nonprofit activity of the Communication Department at Loyola University Maryland.

Using state-of-the-art technology and an experiential learning model of education, Apprentice House publishes books in untraditional ways. This dual responsibility as publishers and educators creates an unprecedented collaborative environment among faculty and students, while teaching tomorrow's editors, designers, and marketers.

Outside of class, progress on book projects is carried forth by the AH Book Publishing Club, a co-curricular campus organization supported by Loyola University Maryland's Office of Student Activities.

Eclectic and provocative, Apprentice House titles intend to entertain as well as spark dialogue on a variety of topics. Financial contributions to sustain the press's work are welcomed. Contributions are tax deductible to the fullest extent allowed by the IRS.

To learn more about Apprentice House books or to obtain submission guidelines, please visit www.apprenticehouse.com.

Apprentice House
Communication Department
Loyola University Maryland
4501 N. Charles Street
Baltimore, MD 21210
Ph: 410-617-5265 • Fax: 410-617-2198
info@apprenticehouse.com•www.apprenticehouse.com

CPSIA information can be obtained
at www.ICGtesting.com
Printed in the USA
FSHW012201110519
58063FS